MAKING 8-BIT ARCADE GAMES IN C

An 8bitworkshop Book

by Steven Hugg

Making 8-Bit Arcade Games in C
Copyright ©2017-2022 by Steven Hugg

All rights reserved. No part of this book may be reproduced without written permission from the author.

Disclaimer
Although every precaution has been taken in the preparation of this book, the publisher and author assume no responsibility for errors or omissions, nor is any liability assumed for damages resulting from the use of the information contained herein. No warranties of any kind are expressed or implied.

Making 8-Bit Arcade Games in C is an independent publication and has not been authorized, sponsored, or otherwise approved by any third party.

Trademarks
Brands and product names mentioned in this work are trademarks or service marks of their respective companies. Use of a term in this work should not be regarded as affecting the validity of any trademark or service mark.

Inquiries
Please refer all inquiries to info@8bitworkshop.com.

Contents

Preface ix
    Why read this book? ix
    Why focus on arcade games? ix
    Which hardware was most influential? x
    Why use C on an 8-bit platform? xi

1 CPU Basics 1
    1.1 Bits, Bytes, and Binary 1
    1.2 Hexadecimal Notation 2
    1.3 Signed vs. Unsigned Bytes 3
    1.4 Integer Overflow and Arithmetic 4
    1.5 The CPU and the Bus 4
    1.6 CPU Instructions 6

2 The Z80 CPU 9
    2.1 Registers 10
    2.2 Reading and Writing Memory 12
    2.3 Flags and Branching 13
    2.4 Stack 16
    2.5 Logical Operations 17

3 Hello 8-bit C World 19
    3.1 Preprocessor and Compiler 19
    3.2 Assembler 22
    3.3 Linker 23
    3.4 ROM Image 25

4 Some C Examples 27

Contents

- 5 The 8bitworkshop C IDE 33
  - 5.1 Debug Window 36
- 6 The VIC Dual Hardware 37
  - 6.1 History 37
  - 6.2 Memory Map 38
  - 6.3 Video 38
  - 6.4 Colors 41
  - 6.5 Typedefs 43
  - 6.6 A Minimal Main Function 44
  - 6.7 C Routines 46
  - 6.8 Controllers 47
  - 6.9 Z80 Entry Routine 49
- 7 Siege Game 51
  - 7.1 Data Structures 52
  - 7.2 Main Function 53
- 8 Shift and Rotate 61
  - 8.1 Shift Operations 61
- 9 The Programmable Sound Generator 65
  - 9.1 The AY-3-8910 PSG 66
  - 9.2 Inline Functions 70
- 10 Binary-Coded Decimal 71
- 11 Pointers 73
  - 11.1 A Pointer is a Typed Memory Address 73
  - 11.2 A Pointer is a Reference To Another Variable ... 74
  - 11.3 A Pointer is a String 74
  - 11.4 A Pointer is an Array ... Sort Of 75
  - 11.5 A Pointer is an Extra Return Value 76
- 12 The Midway 8080 Hardware 77
  - 12.1 History 77
  - 12.2 Memory Map 78
  - 12.3 Graphics 78
  - 12.4 Draw vs. Erase vs. XOR 80

Contents

- 12.5 Drawing Text 82
- 12.6 Pixel-Accurate Sprite Shifting 83
- 12.7 Watchdog Timer 85

13 Game: Cosmic Impalas 87
- 13.1 Game Data 87
- 13.2 The Game Loop 89
- 13.3 Collision Detection 92
- 13.4 Animating an Explosion 95

14 Interrupts 97
- 14.1 Interrupts 97

15 Randomness 101
- 15.1 Galois LFSR 102
- 15.2 Entropy 103

16 Initializing Memory 105
- 16.1 Initialized vs. Uninitialized vs. Const 105
- 16.2 Initializing Memory 107
- 16.3 Initializing Strings vs. Arrays 108

17 The Galaxian Hardware 109
- 17.1 History 109
- 17.2 Memory Map 111
- 17.3 Other Special Addresses 115
- 17.4 Graphics ROMs 116
- 17.5 Sound 116
- 17.6 When Not to Use memset() 117

18 Game: Solarian 119
- 18.1 Drawing Tiles vs. Sprites 121
- 18.2 Attack! 123
- 18.3 Directions and Trig 125
- 18.4 Alien Behavior 127
- 18.5 Returning To Formation 128
- 18.6 Missiles 129
- 18.7 Blowing Up Aliens 130
- 18.8 Game Sound 131

Contents

    18.9 Keeping in Sync with Interrupts 132

19 Making Music 135
    19.1 Hitting the Right Note 135
    19.2 Laying out the Score 136
    19.3 Swinging with the Tempo 137
    19.4 Composing the Music 139
    19.5 Need Some MIDI Files? 139
    19.6 Scramble/Frogger Sound Board 140

20 Integers and You 141
    20.1 Powers of Two 141
    20.2 Unsigned Comparisons 143

21 The Atari Vector Hardware 145
    21.1 History 145
    21.2 How Vector Monitors Work 146
    21.3 Analog Vector Generator (AVG) 147
    21.4 Z80 Memory Map 150
    21.5 AVG C Routines 151

22 3-D Vectors 155
    22.1 3D Types 155
    22.2 Sine and Cosine 157
    22.3 Wireframe Models 159
    22.4 Transformation 161
    22.5 The Mult Box 161

23 Game: Crowded Orbit 163
    23.1 Shape Prerendering 163
    23.2 Actors 165
    23.3 Drawing Actors 166
    23.4 Moving Actors 167
    23.5 Allocating Memory with malloc() 168
    23.6 Linked Lists 169
    23.7 Function Pointers 171
    23.8 Deleting Objects 172
    23.9 Collision Detection 173
    23.10 The Main Loop 174

Contents

- 24 The POKEY Sound Chip 177
  - 24.1 Memory Map 178
  - 24.2 AUDCTL Bit Map 178
  - 24.3 AUDCx Bit Map 178
  - 24.4 Setting AUDF Frequency 179
  - 24.5 POKEY Music 180

- 25 Miscellaneous C Topics 181
  - 25.1 Unions 181
  - 25.2 Big Numbers 182
  - 25.3 Advanced Loop Handling 182
  - 25.4 Operator Precedence 183

- 26 Williams Hardware 185
  - 26.1 History 185
  - 26.2 Memory Map 186
  - 26.3 Bankswitched RAM/ROM 187
  - 26.4 Video Frame Buffer 187
  - 26.5 Palette 188
  - 26.6 Bit Blitter 189
  - 26.7 Blitting to Pixel Boundaries 194
  - 26.8 Other Hardware Locations 194
  - 26.9 When Not to Use memset() 195

- 27 Williams Sprites 197
  - 27.1 Keeping Track of Objects 197
  - 27.2 Getting Rid of Flicker 198
  - 27.3 Collision Detection 200
  - 27.4 Clipping 202
  - 27.5 Getting By With 8 Bits 202

- 28 Run-Length Encoding 203

- 29 Williams Sound 207
  - 29.1 The SWAVE System 208
  - 29.2 Triggering Sounds from the Main CPU 210

- 30 Importing Assets 211
  - 30.1 Installing 8bitworkshop Tools 211

Contents

    30.2 Graphics Tools 214
    30.3 Sound Tools 215
    30.4 Third-Party Tools 215
    30.5 Free Art 215
    30.6 Using 8bitworkshop Offline 216

31 Distributing Your Game 217
    31.1 Making ROM Files 217
    31.2 Playing on Actual Hardware 218

Appendix A: Troubleshooting i
    Programmer Error i
    Compiler Oddities ii

Bibliography iii

Index v

Preface

Why read this book?

1. You want to learn about the internals of Golden Age arcade games.
2. You want to experience what it would have been like to program these games if you had access to an advanced 8-bit C compiler.
3. You want to learn C on devices with slow CPUs and little RAM.

You'll learn all about the hardware of late 1970s-early 1980s arcade games, and we'll create a few simple games with the C programming language along the way.

Why focus on arcade games?

The arcade games developed in the late 1970s to early 1980s demonstrate a wide range of capabilities that evolved over a relatively short period of time. Memory and ROM space got bigger, and video hardware got more sophisticated. Sound evolved too, from bleeps and bloops to FM and speech synthesis.

These architectures were even more stripped down than personal computers of the time, in some ways. Things like extensibility and ease of programming were not design criteria. All of the magic was in the video hardware and sound board, which were a few years ahead of technology available for the home.

Preface

All of the system architectures described in this book were used for more than one title. Some games were developed by the original manufacturer or their licensees, but some were developed unofficially — "bootlegs," in other words. Bootleg vendors could easily duplicate the PCB, made easier by the fact that most arcade games included their own schematic in the service manual. Then it was a matter of reverse-engineering the original ROM and adapting to the new hardware.

Emulator developers have pretty much figured out the hardware by now, but with this book you can experience the thrill of writing your own "unauthorized" homebrew game for an obsolete hardware platform!

Which hardware was most influential?

We're going to focus on five distinct arcade *platforms* — hardware that was repurposed for several different games. Each was influentual or groundbreaking in its own way:

Midway 8080 (1975-1980): Developed by Dave Nutting Associates, this platform's 7 kilobyte frame buffer not only powered the hugely influential *Space Invaders*, but also a couple of dozen other games. Credited as the first arcade platform that used a microprocessor.

VIC Dual (Sega/Gremlin, 1977-1981): A tile-based Z80 platform that drove 20 titles, including some of the first RGB color games. Included for its simplicity and historic value.

Galaxian hardware (Namco, 1979-1984): *Galaxian* was influential game for its vivid RGB color, smooth sprites, and sparkling starfield background. It influenced or formed the basis of several other hardware designs, including *Pac-Man*, *Frogger*, and *Donkey Kong*.

Atari vector hardware (Atari, 1979-1985): The most successful vector-based platform started in black-and-white (*Lunar Lander*) and later moved to color (*Tempest, Star Wars*). It used a Motorola 6502 or 6809 CPU with custom hardware to draw vectors and calcuate 3D transformations.

Why use C on an 8-bit platform?

Williams hardware (Williams, 1980-1986): This 6809-based platform used a whopping 36K of memory for its 16-color frame buffer, and featured custom GPU chips that drew sprites at impressive speeds. The dedicated sound CPU, developed first for pinball machines, produced some interesting noises.

Why use C on an 8-bit platform?

This is a good question, because it isn't always a good idea. Using C isn't practical on the Atari 2600, for instance, because of the small amount of RAM/ROM space available and the precise timing required. (You could get away with writing some non-time-critical routines in C, though they'd be less efficient.)

It wasn't uncommon for programmers to annotate their printed code in pen, handing the reams of paper to someone to input the changes into a primitive line editor, or even typing out punch cards to feed into a PDP assembler. Others would skip the tools, poking machine code directly into an emulator, inviting the fates to deliver a power outage and undo their work.

They certainly were not using C compilers back then — *The C Programming Language* by Kernighan & Ritchie was published in 1978, the same year *Space Invaders* was rolling off production lines. C was relevant in the academic UNIX world, but otherwise it was just another programming language among many.

However, we do have modern compiler technology on our side, and for this book we'll be using a fantastic open-source compiler called SDCC (Small Device C Compiler) which supports the Z80 chip and has lots of clever optimizations. It isn't as fast as hand-rolled assembler, but it's a lot easier to write. You'll still get a taste of the limitations that make 8-bit game programming challenging.

Figure 1: Galaxian arcade system board (photo by Dennis van Zuijlekom, CC BY-SA 2.0)

1
CPU Basics

> Note: If you're already familiar with 8-bit CPUs, or you've read my previous book *Making Games for the Atari 2600*, you can safely skip to the next chapter.

1.1 Bits, Bytes, and Binary

All digital computers operate on bits and bytes. Let's review a few things about them.

A *bit* is a binary value — it can be either zero (0) or one (1). We might also say it is off/on, or false/true. The important thing is that it can only have one of two values.

A *byte* is an ordered sequence of eight (8) bits. There's nothing special about the number 8; it's just a convenient standard.[1] We say a computer has an *8-bit architecture* if it primarily manipulates bytes.

We can create a written representation of a byte in *binary notation*, which just lists the bits from left to right, for example: %00011011. We can then shorten the byte notation by removing the leading zeros, giving us %11011. The % denotes a binary number, and we'll use this notation throughout the book.

---

[1] The first microprocessors were used in computer terminals, and an 8-bit standard worked nicely with the ASCII character set.

1. CPU Basics

The eight bits in a byte are not just independent ones and zeros; they can also express numbers. We assign values to each bit and then add them up. The least-significant bit, the rightmost (our index starts at zero, i.e. *bit 0*), has a value of 1. For each position to the left, the value increases by a power of two until we reach the most-significant bit, the leftmost (*bit 7*) with a value of 128.

Here are the values for an entire byte:

Bit #	7	6	5	4	3	2	1	0
Value	128	64	32	16	8	4	2	1

Let's line up our example byte, %11011, with these values:

Bit #	7	6	5	4	3	2	1	0
Value	128	64	32	16	8	4	2	1
Our Byte	0	0	0	1	1	0	1	1
Bit*Value				16	8		2	1

When we add up all the bit values, we get $16 + 8 + 2 + 1 = 27$.

A binary number with N bits has 2^N unique combinations, so an 8-bit number can represent 256 different values including zero.

1.2 Hexadecimal Notation

Binary notation can be unwieldy, so it's common to represent bytes using *hexadecimal notation*, or *base 16*. We split the byte into two 4-bit halves, or *nibbles*. We treat each nibble as a separate value from 0 to 15, like this:

Bit #	7	6	5	4	3	2	1	0
Value	8	4	2	1	8	4	2	1

We then convert each 4-bit nibble's value to a symbol — 0-9 remains 0 through 9, but 10-15 becomes A through F.

Let's convert the binary number %11011 and see how it would be represented in hexadecimal:

Bit #	7	6	5	4	3	2	1	0
Value	8	4	2	1	8	4	2	1
Our Byte	0	0	0	1	1	0	1	1
Bit*Value				1	8		2	1
Decimal Value	1				11			
Hex Value	1				B			

We see in the above table that the decimal number 27, represented as %11011 in binary, becomes $1B in hexadecimal format.

> The "$" prefix indicates a hexadecimal number. In C programs, you'll see hex numbers prefixed by "0x", e.g. 0x1b or 0xAA. We'll use these two notations interchangeably in this book.

1.3 Signed vs. Unsigned Bytes

One more thing about bytes: We've described how they can be interpreted as any value from 0 through 255, or an *unsigned* value. We can also interpret them as negative or *signed* quantities.

This requires a trick known as *two's complement* arithmetic. If the high bit is 1 (in other words, if the unsigned value is 128 or greater), we treat the value as negative, as if we had subtracted 256 from it:

```
 0-127 ($00-$7F):     positive
128-255 ($80-$FF):    negative (value - 256)
```

Note that there's nothing in the byte identifying it as signed — it's all in how you interpret it, as we'll see later.

1. CPU Basics

1.4 Integer Overflow and Arithmetic

Since the numbers we deal with in 8-bit CPUs are so small, *integer overflow* is a thing we'll have to deal with often.

When you add two numbers, the CPU adds them just like you would by hand, but in binary. Each binary digit is added, and if you have to carry the 1 (which only happens when adding the bits 1 and 1) you carry it to the next bit. An example:

Bit #		7	6	5	4	3	2	1	0
Byte A +		1	0	1	0	0	1	0	1
Byte B +		1	0	1	1	0	1	1	0
Carry	1		1			1			
=		0	1	0	1	1	0	1	1

Table 1.1: Binary Addition of Two Bytes With Carry

What happens to that extra carry bit? We only have 8 bits in a byte, so the result of the addition is *truncated* to 8 bits. We also could call this an *integer overflow*. The carry bit is retained in the CPU's Carry flag, and could be used by future calculations or just discarded.

An unsigned byte can only represent the values 0 to 255, so if $a + b >= 256$ then the 8-bit result is $(a + b)$ mod 256 (mod is the *modulus* operator, which is basically the remainder of a division.) For 16-bit unsigned numbers, it'd be $(a + b)$ mod 2^{16} (65536).

The overflow behavior actually makes integer subtractions work. The number -1 can be expressed as the signed byte $FF (255). The result of $a + 255$ is $(a + 255)$ mod 256, which is the same as adding -1 to a.

1.5 The CPU and the Bus

Think of the CPU as an intricate timepiece. An electronic spring unwinds and an internal clock ticks millions of times per second. On every tick, electrons turn tiny gears, and the

1.5. The CPU and the Bus

CPU comes to rest in a different state. Each tick is called a *clock cycle*, or *CPU clock*.

All the CPU does is execute instructions, one after another. It fetches an instruction (reads it from memory), decodes it (figures out what to do) and then executes it (does some things in a prescribed order). Each instruction may take several clock cycles to execute, each clock cycle performing a specific step. The CPU then figures out which instruction to grab next, and repeats the process.

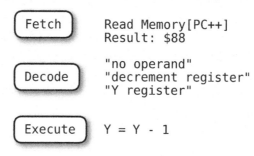

Figure 1.1: CPU Cycle

During each clock cycle, the CPU can read from or write to the bus. The bus is a set of "lanes" where each lane can hold a single bit at a time. In a 8-bit processor, the *data bus* is eight bits (one byte) wide.

Devices like memory, sound synths, and video generators are attached to the bus, and receive read and write signals. The CPU doesn't know which devices are connected to the bus – all it knows is that it either receives eight bits back from a read, or sends eight bits out into the world during a write.

As bytes are read into the CPU, they are temporarily stored in *registers*, where they can be manipulated further or written back out into the world.

1. CPU Basics

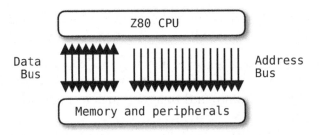

Figure 1.2: Bus

Besides the 8-bit data bus, our CPU has a 16-bit *address bus*. The address bus describes "where" and the data bus describes "what." Since the address bus is 16 bits wide, this gives us 65,536 possible addresses that we can target, each address representing a single byte.

1.6 CPU Instructions

Let's look at what happens when the CPU executes this LD (Load) instruction:

    ld   a,(#0x1234)

This tells the CPU to load the 8-bit register A with the value found at address $1234.

The CPU will set the 16 pins on the address bus to the binary encoding for $1234, set the read/write pins to "read memory," and wait for a response on the data bus.

Devices on the bus look at the address $1234 and determine whether the message is for them – by design, only one device should respond. The CPU then reads the value from the data bus and puts it in the A register.

If we just swap the two operands, we now have a LD instruction that writes to memory:

    ld   (#0x1234),a

The CPU will set the address bus to $1234 and the data bus to whatever is in the A register, then set the read/write pins to

1.6. CPU Instructions

"write memory." Again, the bus devices look at the address bus and the write signal and decide if they should listen or ignore it.

Let's say a memory chip responds – the memory chip would read the 8-bit value off the data bus and store it in the memory cell corresponding to address $1234. The CPU does not get a response from a write; it just assumes everything worked out fine.

The example CPU instructions we've seen so far have been in a human-readable language called *assembly language*. The CPU isn't fluent in this language, but it understands a compact code called *machine code*. A program called an *assembler* takes the human-readable assembly code and produces machine code. For example:

    ld   a,(#0x1234)   -> 3A 34 12

This assembly instruction translates to three bytes of machine code: $3A, $34, and $12. $3A is the *opcode* which determines the instruction and *addressing mode*. $34 and $12 are part of the *operand*, which in this case is a 16-bit number spanning two bytes.

> You'll note that when we split the 16-bit value $1234 into bytes, the $34 is first and the $12 is second – this is because our CPU is a *little-endian* processor, expecting the least-significant parts of multibyte numbers first.
>
> The least-significant byte (LSB) is also called the low byte, while the most-significant byte (MSB) is also called the high byte.

2
The Z80 CPU

Figure 2.1: Zilog Z80 (photo by Gennadiy Shvets, CC BY 2.5)

Throughout most of the 1970s, CPUs were still prohibitively expensive for arcade games, at costs of hundreds of dollars per unit. Thus, many early arcade games were built without CPUs — just custom discrete circuits. For example, Atari's original Pong game contained 66 microchips wired together on a custom *PCB* (Printed Circuit Board). These components implemented the entire game logic, video signal, and sound.

The Intel 8080 CPU cost around $100 per unit at this time, and competitors were eager to get in on the market. Federico Faggin defected from Intel to found Zilog and develop the Z80 CPU, a souped-up version of the 8080. It would be used as the basis for many home computers and video game consoles, as well as coin-operated arcade games (the subject of this book!)

Compared to the much-cheaper MOS 6502, the Z80 was more powerful and complex. It had many more registers – seven 16-bit registers and four alternate registers compared to the 6502's

2. The Z80 CPU

five 8-bit registers. It could add and subtract 16-bit values, which on the 6502 had to be done in separate 8-bit instructions. It also had block memory, I/O, and search instructions, which could operate on multiple values with a single instruction.

Whereas the 6502 mapped both memory and I/O devices into a single 64k space, the Z80 separated the two. The IN and OUT instructions perform input and output, while instructions like LD perform memory operations. Still, some system designers opted to ignore the I/O instructions and mapped everything into memory space anyway.

The Z80's original clock speed was 2.5 MHz, which seems much faster than the 6502's 1 MHz — but instructions on the Z80 take at least twice as many cycles as the 6502, so the clock increase is not as significant as it may seem.

2.1 Registers

The Z80 has eight 16-bit *registers*, each identified by a two-letter pair. Each register pair has its own "personality", which corresponds to the kinds of CPU instructions available to it:

AF - This pair's 8-bit registers are usually treated separately. The A register is the *accumulator* and is used by many instructions. F is the *flags* register and its bits are cleared and set depending on the results of instructions.

BC - General-purpose 16-bit register. Can load/store memory to/from A only.

DE - Another general-purpose 16-bit register.

HL - Useful for 16-bit arithmetic operations, can also use any 8-bit register for read/write operations.

The 8-bit components of each of the above can be addressed separately; for example, B is the low byte (least significant byte) of the BC register.

2.1. Registers

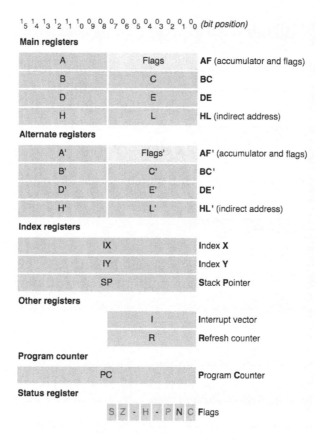

Figure 2.2: Z80 Registers[1]

The other 16-bit registers are as follows:

PC - The *Program Counter*. It holds the address of the currently executing instruction.

SP - The *Stack Pointer*. It holds the current address of the top of the stack, and is used by the PUSH and POP operations, as well as CALL and RET.

IX - An *index register*, which is used for addressing modes like (IX+register). Our C compiler reserves it as the frame pointer.

IY - Another index register. The compiler uses it to hold memory addresses.

11

2. The Z80 CPU

IR - Interrupt and Refresh registers. Special-purpose, not generally used for computing.

There are also four alternate (shadow) registers for AF, BC, DE, and HL. They can be quickly swapped with the EX and EXX instructions. This is useful for interrupt routines.

2.2 Reading and Writing Memory

Take the following C statement, which assigns one 8-bit variable to another:

```
lives = maxlives;
```

Let's look at the C compiler's assembly output. This simple assignment statement requires multiple LD instructions:

```
ld      a,(#_maxlives)
ld      (#_lives),a
```

The first LD reads from the address of the maxlives variable into the A register. The second LD then writes the A register contents to the address of the lives variable.

Let's say we wanted to subtract one life (again in C):

```
lives--;
```

The compiler uses the DEC instruction, which decrements its operand by 1:

```
ld      hl,#_lives
dec     (hl)
```

The DEC instruction can only access memory through a register. So this code first loads the HL register with the address of the lives variable, then uses the DEC instruction with the (HL) *addressing mode*. This decrements the value at the address in the HL register.

2.3. Flags and Branching

The ADD/ADC and SUB/SBC instructions handle addition and subtraction. Things get more complicated when going beyond 8-bit values. Let's say we want to add 100 to the 16-bit score variable:

```
score += 100;
```

Since score is a 16-bit value, the compiler has two additions to make: First it must add 100 ($64 in hex) to the low byte of score, and then add the carry bit to the high byte (we covered binary-addition-with-carry in Chapter 1):

```
_add_100_points::
        ld      hl,#_score
        ld      a,(hl)          ; load lo byte of score
        add     a, #0x64        ; add lo byte
        ld      (hl),a          ; store lo byte of result
        inc     hl
        ld      a,(hl)          ; load hi byte of score
        adc     a, #0x00        ; add hi byte
        ld      (hl),a          ; store hi byte of result
        ret
```

For the first addition, HL is loaded with the address of the score variable's low byte, and ADD is used to add the value to the low byte. (As described earlier, Z80 is *little-endian*, which means the least-significant bytes come first in memory.) The INC HL moves HL to the high byte. Then the second addition takes place, using ADC to add the Carry bit.

2.3 Flags and Branching

The bits of the F register correspond to various *flags*. They are changed when an instruction executes, according to the result of the calculation. Some instructions change them in different ways, and some (like LD) do not change them at all.

2. The Z80 CPU

Bit	Flag	Flag Name	Flag Description
0	C	Carry	Result overflowed register
1	N	Add/Subtract	Last op was subtraction
2	V	Parity/Overflow	Signed result overflow, or even number of bits
3			
4	H	Half-Carry	Carry bit 3 to bit 4
5			
6	Z	Zero	Result was zero
7	S	Signed	Result is negative

The CPU keeps the address of the current instruction in a 16-bit register called the *Program Counter (PC)*. Typically, the CPU reads an instruction and increments the PC to the next instruction, but some instructions change the PC. These are called *branch* or *jump* instructions. Jumps can be conditional, which means that the jump may or may not be taken depending on whether a given CPU flag is set.

The flags are often used to check for specific conditions. For example, this C statement checks to see if we have any more lives left, and calls end_game if the number of lives is zero:

```
if (lives == 0) {
  end_game();
}
```

This is the compiled output:

```
_check_lives::
    ld    a,(#_lives)     ; load A with lives
    or    a, a            ; set zero flag
    ret   NZ              ; return if not zero
    jp    _end_game       ; if zero, end game
```

It first loads the lives variable into A. Next, it uses the OR instruction to set the flags, by OR-ing a register with itself (which changes nothing except the flags.) The RET NZ instruction checks the Z flag, and returns if it is *not* set. Otherwise execution proceeds to the JP instruction, and we transfer control to the end_game function.

14

2.3. Flags and Branching

The branch instructions are also good for writing loops. Let's say we wanted to count from 0 to 99, and to write each value in sequence to an I/O port:

```
char i;
for (i=0; i<100; i++) {
  output_port = i;
}
```

The compiled output uses the LD and INC instructions, and the OUT instruction to write to the I/O port. The SUB and JR instructions are responsible for implementing the loop:

```
_write_loop::
        ld      d,#0x00
repeat:
        ld      a,d
        out     (_output_port),a    ; write to port
        inc     d
        ld      a,d
        sub     a, #0x64            ; set flags for (d-100)
        jr      C,repeat            ; if carry set, repeat
        ret
```

The loop variable is kept in the D register. When it gets below 0x64 (100 decimal), the SUB instruction will set the Carry flag. The following JR C,<label> instruction transfers control back to the repeat label as long as the Carry flag is set. So as long as D is below 100, the loop will repeat.

15

2.4 Stack

The Z80 also has a *Stack Pointer (SP)*, which is typically is set at program startup to point somewhere in RAM. The stack has many uses — it stores temporary values, passes function parameters, and it keeps the return address when a function is called.

The PUSH instruction pushes a 16-bit register onto the stack. This decrements SP by 2 and then writes the register to the address at SP. (We say the stack *grows downward* because memory addresses decrease as items are pushed.)

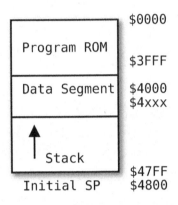

Figure 2.3: Example of a Z80 memory map

The POP instruction restores the last thing PUSHed. It reads the 16-bit value at SP to a register, and then increments SP by 2.

When calling a function, the CALL instruction pushes the current Program Counter onto the stack. The C compiler also keeps a lot of other stuff in the stack, including local variables and function parameters. All this stuff is referred to as the *stack frame* of the function.

Let's write a function that has a single 16-bit parameter, and adds it to the current score:

```c
void add_score(int amount) {
    score += amount;
}
```

If we called this function with the statement add_score(100), this code would execute the call:

```
        ld      hl,#0x0064
        push    hl              ; push argument = 100
        call    _add_score
        pop     af              ; pop argument
```

The caller loads 100 into HL, pushes it onto the stack, then calls add_score. In this C compiler, the caller is responsible for cleaning up the stack, so after the CALL returns it does a POP to discard the value it pushed.

2.5 Logical Operations

The "logical" instructions combine the bits of two operands, performing a bit (logic) operation on each bit:

AND	A & B	Set bit if A and B are set.
OR	A | B	Set bit if A or B (or both) are set.
XOR	A ^ B	Set bit if either A or B are set, but not both (exclusive-or).

For example, let's AND a byte variable with the constant $1F:

```
xpos &= 0x1f;
```

For AND, if a bit was set in both the A register and the operand, it'll be set in A after the instruction executes. Let's say xpos is initially $75:

```
        $75  01110101
AND     $1F  00011111
-------------------
        $15  00010101
```

The AND operation is useful for limiting the range of a value. For example, AND #$1F is the same as (A mod 32), and the result will have a range of 0 to 31.

What if we did an OR instead?

```
xpos |= 0x1f;
```

OR sets bits if they are set in either A or the operand, i.e. unless they are clear in both.

2. THE Z80 CPU

```
        $55    01010101
OR      $1F    00011111
---------------------
        $5F    01011111
```

Sometimes the compiler emits OR A,A just to set the flags, usually to see if A is zero. Similarly, OR A,L tests the 16-bit AL register for zero.

What about an XOR?

```
  xpos ^= 0x1f;
```

XOR (exclusive-or) is like an OR, except that bits that are set in both A and the operand are cleared.

```
        $55    01010101
XOR     $1F    00011111
---------------------
        $4A    01001010
```

Note that if we do the same XOR twice, we get the original value back.

In addition, the SET, RES, and BIT instructions set, clear, and test individual bits.

3

Hello 8-bit C World

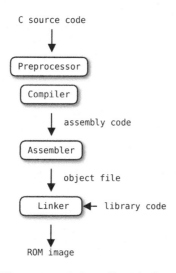

Figure 3.1: C Compiler Pipeline

Since this book is about programming to the bare metal of the hardware, we're going to dissect a simple C program all the way to the bytes of the machine code.

First, let's talk about the C compiler *pipeline* — the several steps that are needed to turn your source code into a final ROM image that is loaded into the machine.

3.1 Preprocessor and Compiler

Most programming tutorials include a simple "Hello, World!" example, which outputs a single line of text to the console. In keeping with this tradition, this will be our sample C program for this chapter:

```
#include <stdio.h>

void main() {
  printf("HELLO WORLD"); // output some text
}
```

3. Hello 8-bit C World

> To see it on 8bitworkshop.com: Select the **VIC Dual** platform, then select the **Hello World** file.

The first line is a *preprocessor directive*, indicated by a hash (#) at the start of the line:

#include <stdio.h>

The *preprocessor* is the first thing that touches the C source code. One of its primary jobs is to include *header files* into the source, which contain various C declarations and macro definitions. This is pretty much how C implements modules or library routines.

The other primary job is *macro expansion*. Your C source (or included files) can contain *macro definitions*, which tell the preprocessor to substitute one string for another, with optional parameters. It's common to use these for constant values, for example:

#define EXTRA_LIFE_SCORE 10000

You can also use them for complex expressions, code generation, and all sorts of other mischief. We'll cover some practical uses of macros later on.

Anyway, our #include directive tells the preprocessor to include the text of the standard header file stdio.h into the code. This gives us, among other things, the declaration of the printf function which we can now use.

> *return-type function-name(param1, param2...)*
>
> Declares or defines a function.

In C, all code statements must be placed inside of a *function*. We're going to define a function called main, which is traditionally the first to run when a C program starts:

3.1. Preprocessor and Compiler

```
void main() {
  printf("HELLO WORLD"); // output some text
}
```

`void main()` is the *declaration* of the function. `main` is an *identifier*, which is a fancy term for "name of something." `void` is the *return type* of the function — our function doesn't return a value, so its type is `void`.

> In C, all identifiers must begin with a letter or underscore. Subsequent characters may also contain the digits 0-9.

Any identifier used in a program must be declared first, so that the compiler knows its type. This declaration tells the compiler that `main` is a function taking no arguments (the `()` after the identifier) and that it returns `void` (i.e. no value).

Identifiers in C are case-sensitive, which means if you change the case of just one letter of an identifier, it's a different identifier.

> *function-name(argument1, argument2...);*
>
> Calls a function.

Following the curly brackets is the `function body`, which contains a list of declarations (e.g. local variables) and then a list of statements. There are no declarations, and just a single statement — a *function call* to `printf`. We pass it a string argument in double quotes, which tells it to print "HELLO, WORLD!" to the console. Finally, a semicolon marks the end of the statement.

One more thing: The `//` indicates the start of a *line comment*. When the preprocessor sees two slashes, it omits everything until the end of the line. There are also *multi-line comments*, which look like this:

```
/* this comment can take up
   multiple lines */
```

3.2 Assembler

The compiler spits out a bunch of files, the most important of which is the *assembly listing*. This is our C program translated into not-quite-final Z80 code. It's not critical to understand it thoroughly, but let's briefly review it.

Here's a quick guide on what the columns mean:

```
OFFSET BYTES          CYCLES LINE#
  011C 3A 34 12        [10]    42        ld      a,(#0x1234)

OFFSET - The ROM offset, in hex
BYTES  - The bytes of the instruction, in hex
CYCLES - The # of CPU cycles taken by the instruction
LINE#  - The line number in the assembly output
```

The compiled `main` function is pretty simple as far as C functions go. The first line is a label (`_main::`) which marks the start of the function for the assembler. Note that it is prepended with an underscore; this is standard practice for C symbols:

```
  0000                  56 _main::
```

The first instruction loads the 16-bit register HL with the constant value `___str_0`, which is the address of the "HELLO WORLD" string:

```
  0000 21 ?? ??         [10]    58      ld      hl,#___str_0
```

Why the "?? ??" in our listing? That's because we don't know the address of the string yet. The linker will figure that out in the next step of the pipeline.

Now that the the HL register contains the address of our string, we want to pass it as an argument to the `printf` function. So we push it to the stack:

3.3. Linker

```
0003 E5            [11]    59         push   hl
```

Now we call the _printf function, which does its business and returns. It places a return value on the stack, which we've ignored in the C code — but the compiler knows it's there, so it does a pop to get rid of it:

```
0004 CD ?? ??      [17]    60         call   _printf
0007 F1            [10]    61         pop    af
```

Now we've reached the end of our main function, and we return with the ret instruction: [1]

```
0008 C9            [10]    62         ret
```

One more thing we forgot — where's the ___str_0 label defined? The compiler defined it right after the function, and defined all the bytes of our "HELLO WORLD" string, too:

```
0009                       63 ___str_0:
0009 48 45 4C 4C 4F 20     64         .ascii "HELLO WORLD"
     57 4F 52 4C 44
0014 00                    65         .db 0x00
```

Note the 0x00 at the end of the string; this is called a null-terminated or C-style string. C functions generally recognize that a zero signals the end of a string. Unfortunately, this means you can't use a zero value as part of a string, but that doesn't usually come up in textual data.

3.3 Linker

The assembler spits out another bunch of files, the most important being the *object code* for our C source file. This contains the bytes of the Z80 machine code, plus some extra stuff to help the linker. So far the object code is *relocatable*, meaning it can run at

---

[1]On a system like UNIX, this would return control to the command prompt. On an arcade game, you'd probably loop forever inside of main().

23

any location in memory. After the linker runs, all code will be fixed to a particular location.

The linker's job is to output a ROM-ready machine code image that the CPU can execute directly. It does this by combining your compiled object files with external libraries, and applying *fixups* to unresolved addresses to that they point to the correct final memory locations.

Note that we had two unresolved addresses, ___str_0 and _printf. The first identifier is an internal reference, which the linker easily resolves:

```
0000 21 09 00        [10]    58          ld       hl,#___str_0
```

The second identifier, _printf, is an external *library function*. The linker has to look up the identifier in an external file (included with the compiler) and include the function in the final image, as well as all of the functions on which it depends. Sometimes this can be an awful lot of code!

Here's our final code listing with all the fixups applied:

```
0000                         56   _main::
0000 21 09 00        [10]    58         ld       hl,#___str_0
0003 E5              [11]    59         push     hl
0004 CD 41 00        [17]    60         call     _printf
0007 F1              [10]    61         pop      af
0008 C9              [10]    62         ret
0009                         63   ___str_0:
0009 48 45 4C 4C 4F 20       64         .ascii   "HELLO WORLD"
     57 4F 52 4C 44
0014 00                      65         .db      0x00
```

You may even pull in external functions without realizing it. For example, the Z80 has no multiplication or division instruction, so the C compiler uses external library routines. The same goes for any floating point operations.

3.4 ROM Image

The final ROM image is just the sequence of bytes output by the assembler. On the Z80, the ROM image is usually loaded at address 0, since that's where the CPU starts executing code after a reset.

> **Note: This Example Doesn't Work (Yet!)**
>
> This example won't work out-of-the-box in our Z80 IDE, because our system is a bit more stripped-down than your standard C compiler. We'd have to add a couple of extra things:
>
> **Standard I/O functions:** Although `printf` is defined in the standard library, there's no definition for the `putchar` function which it uses to output characters. We'll have to define `putchar` for the particular display device on our target platform.
>
> **Stack pointer initialization:** When the CPU is reset, it sets the Program Counter (PC) register to 0. This corresponds to the beginning of our `main` function, so it will begin executing it immediately. There's one small problem: the Stack Pointer (SP) register has not yet been set, so when we push/pop values to the stack, the CPU will probably not be addressing a valid region of RAM. This is why most C compilers don't start at `main`, but run an *entry routine* first to set things up. We'll describe this in a future chapter.

4
Some C Examples

Before we get started making arcade games, let's go over some more examples of C code.

> *type name;*
> *type name = initializer;*
>
> Declares a variable named *name* of type *type*, optionally initializing its value.

When you declare a *variable*, you reserve space for it in memory. Here we declare two variables of type char, which is an 8-bit integer type, and initialize one of them:

```
char maxlives = 5;
char lives;
```

These are *global variables* because they are declared outside of a function. They take up memory for the duration of the program, in the *data segment*.

> *x = expr*
>
> Assigns the value of *expr* to the variable *x*.

This C function new_game assigns one 8-bit variable to another, setting the value of lives to 5:

```
void new_game() {
  lives = maxlives;
}
```

> x++
>
> x--
>
> Increment or decrement x by 1.
>
> If this value is used in an expression, x is evaluated *before* the increment takes place.

You might call this function when the player loses a life:

```
void subtract_one_life() {
  lives--;
}
```

> x += *expr*
>
> x -= *expr*
>
> Add or subtract the value *expr* to the variable x.

This function adds 100 points to the score:

```
int score;

void add_100_points() {
  score += 100;
}
```

Functions can also have parameters. Let's write a function that takes a single 16-bit parameter, and adds it to the current score:

```
void add_score(int amount) {
  score += amount;
}
```

> *if* (expr) statement1 else statement2;
>
> If *expr* evaluates to true (non-zero), then execute *statement1*. Otherwise, execute *statement2*.

This function checks to see if we have any more lives left, and calls end_game if the number of lives is equal to zero:

```
void check_lives() {
  if (lives == 0) {
    end_game();
  }
}
```

The double-equals (==) is a *relational operator* that compares two values and evaluates to 1 (true) if they are equal. There's also a not-equal operator (!=) and a host of comparisons (<, <=, >, >=).

> *for* (init; condition; increment) statement;
>
> First evaluate *init*. Then loop while *condition* is true, repeatedly executing *statement* and then the *increment* expression.

Let's say we wanted to count from 0 to 99, and call the function display_number for each value:

```
void display_100_numbers() {
  char i;
  for (i=0; i<100; i++) {
    display_number(i);
  }
}
```

Note that we declared the i variable inside the function. This makes it a *local variable* that takes up space on the stack, temporarily. We can only access it inside of this function.

4. Some C Examples

> ***while** (condition) statement;*
>
> If *condition* evaluates to true, execute *statement* and loop.

We can use a `while` statement to loop until some condition is true. For example:

```
while (player_is_alive) {
  move_player();
}
```

> ***return** expression;*
>
> Exit the function, returning *expression* as the result.

```
byte did_hit_high_score() {
  if (score > high_score) {
    high_score = score;
    return 1;
  } else {
    return 0;
  }
}
```

In C, whitespace doesn't matter (except inside of strings) so the following works just as well:

```
byte did_hit_high_score() {
  if (score > high_score) { high_score = score; return 1; }
  else return 0;
}
```

Note that we've also omitted the brackets around `return 0;` – you can do this for single lone statements, although it's often a good idea to include the brackets for clarity. The compiled code will be the same in either case.

> *a && b*
>
> Logical AND.
> Evaluates *a* and returns 0 if it is false. Evaluates *b* and returns 0 if it is false. Otherwise, returns 1.

> *a || b*
>
> Logical OR.
> Evaluates *a* and returns 1 if it is true. Evaluates *b* and returns 1 if it is true. Otherwise, returns 0.

You can make complex conditional expressions with the *logical operators*.

The && operator means (this AND that):

```
if (button_pressed && bullet_position < 100) {
  fire_bullet();
}
```

The || operator means (this OR that):

```
if (player_1_dead || player_2_dead) {
  end_round();
}
```

These are distinct from the *bitwise operators* (&, |, and ^) in that they only work on boolean values (0 and 1). They also perform *short-circuit evaluation,* meaning they stop evaluating as soon as the result is known.

5

The 8bitworkshop C IDE

In this chapter, we'll discuss the tools we'll use to develop and test our game code. These tools comprise our *interactive development environment*, or IDE.

To start the IDE, visit http://8bitworkshop.com/ in a web browser. For best results, use a recent version of Google Chrome, Mozilla Firefox, or Apple Safari.

The IDE supports all arcade platforms covered in this book. To switch between platforms, click the Menu icon at the upper-left of the page, then choose one from the **Platform** menu, as shown in Figure 5.2.

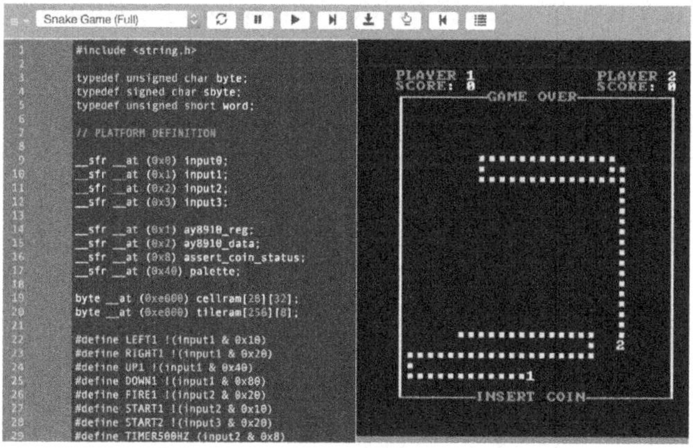

Figure 5.1: 8bitworkshop IDE

5. The 8bitworkshop C IDE

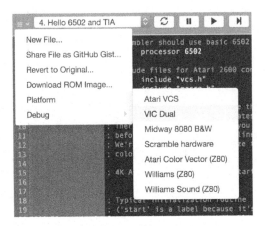

Figure 5.2: IDE platform menu

The IDE is packaged with several example programs. To the right of the menu icon, you can access a pulldown menu that allows you to select a file to load, as shown in Figure 5.3.

You can edit these files as much as you want — all changes are persisted in browser local storage and they'll be there if you close the browser tab and come back. To reset and fully clear your changes, select **Reset to Original** from the menu.

To start from scratch, select **New File** from the menu. Type in the name of your new file, typically with a ".c" extension for C source files. (You can also do Z80 assembler with the ".asm" extension.)

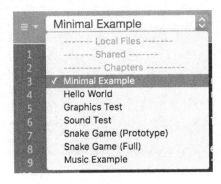

Figure 5.3: IDE file pulldown

To share your file with others, select **Share File as GitHub Gist** from the menu. This will upload your file to the GitHub service, and then show you a link that you can copy to the clipboard. Send this link to others, and they can view and play your source file, making their own local changes if they wish.

The IDE includes an *emulator* for each arcade platform, which runs the code on a simulated arcade machine. To control the game, first click the emulator screen to gain focus. The keyboard commands vary from game-to-game, but they are usually as follows:

- **Arrow keys** - Move
- **Space bar** - Fire button
- 5 - Insert coin
- 1 - Start game (1 player)
- 2 - Start game (2 players)

The other tool is a *C compiler*. The one we use is called SDCC and also runs in the web browser, along with a web-based text editor. Each time you make a change to the code, the IDE immediately compiles it and then sends the final ROM image to the emulator, allowing you to see code changes near-instantly.

The last tool is a simple *debugger* that allows you to step through machine code instructions, view memory, and start and stop the program. The buttons at the top of the screen perform several debugging functions:

- **Reset:** Hard reset the emulator, then single-step to the first instruction.
- **Pause:** Stop the emulator.
- **Run:** Resume the emulator after pausing.
- **Step:** Execute the next CPU intruction, then break.
- **Run To Line:** Set a "breakpoint" on the current line (the one the cursor is on). The emulator will stop when execution reaches that instruction.

5. The 8bitworkshop C IDE

- **Step Out of Subroutine:** Run until the current subroutine returns, then break.
- **Step Backwards:** Step back a single CPU instruction.

- **Show Disassembly:** Show the compiled assembly listing of a C source file.
- **Show Memory:** Show a memory browser (see Figure 5.4).
- **Show Profile:** Show profiling information for each line of source code.

5.1 Debug Window

Whenever the IDE hits a breakpoint or is single-stepped, a debug window appears in the lower-right of the screen. This shows the internal state of the CPU, including all registers and flags.

```
PC 0098    -Z-H-V--
SP E7F7    IR 0070
IX 0000    IY E417
AF 0054    BC 0807
DE E400    HL E7F9
```

> **NOTE:** The IDE is under active development and may differ from what we describe here. The source code is available at https://github.com/sehugg/8bitworkshop.

```
E3E0  0A 05 02 01 80 40 20 10  0B 84 42 21 90 48 24 92   _cellram
E3F0  49 A4 D2 69 34 1A 8D 46  23 11 08 04 82 41 A0 D0   _cellram
E400  0F 17 02 00 00 31 FE 00  09 0B 00 00 00 32 FE 00   _players
E410  01                                                  _attract
E410        09                                            _frames_per_move
E410           00 EF BE AD DE FD  9D                      credits
```

Figure 5.4: Memory browser

6

The VIC Dual Hardware

6.1 History

In 1976, Lane Hauck was getting restless. He had been working on pinball and "wall games" like *Play Ball* and *Trapshoot* at Gremlin Industries, and wanted management to get into the video game business.[2]

He had been messing around with a game called *Blockade* that displayed an arrow on a screen. It could be moved in four directions by pressing switches, and left a trail behind it. The player's goal was to avoid his own trail, and the trails of other players. After it was released, Lane's game was quickly cloned by others — Midway's *Checkmate* for example, which was cited as inspiration for the light cycle sequence in the 1982 *Tron* arcade game.

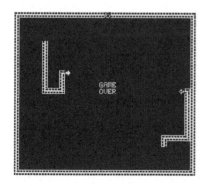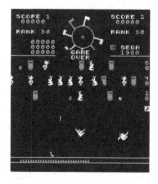

Figure 6.1: Gremlin's "Blockade" (left) and Sega's "Carnival" (right)

6. The VIC Dual Hardware

Later, the company would make *Safari*, which was based on the Z80 chip. After Gremlin's merger with Sega, this "VIC Dual" architecture would be used for 20 or so games through 1981, perhaps the most familiar being *Carnival*. Also notable was *Head On*, a car game which had players eating dots before *Pac-Man* arrived on the scene. All of these games had similar CPU and video circuits, but the sound board could be swapped out.

The VIC Dual system is built around a Z80 running at 1.934 MHz with 8 KB of RAM, most of this shared by the video system.

6.2 Memory Map

Start	End	Description
$0000	$3fff	ROM (16KB)
$8000	$837f	video RAM (cells)
$8380	$87ff	free RAM
$8800	$8fff	video RAM (tiles)

Table 6.1: VIC Dual Memory Map

The address decoder that selects RAM or ROM only looks at the highest bit, so all of the RAM address space is mirrored at $9000, $A000, $B000, $C000, up to $F000. Most 16KB VIC Dual systems also mirror the ROM at $4000-$7FFF.

6.3 Video

The VIC Dual's video generator has more in common with the dumb terminals of the day than later video games. It is based on *cells* and *tiles*. Think of cells as the rows and columns that determine which characters are displayed on your terminal, and tiles as the bitmaps for each character — although we can define the tiles to be any shape, not just letters and numbers.

The video generator can display a 32x28 grid of cells — or 28x32, if the monitor was rotated 90 degrees. Each cell is cell taken from one of 256 8x8 pixel bitmaps, also defined in RAM. Early boards only supported monochrome graphics, but later boards could output 8 different colors.

6.3. Video

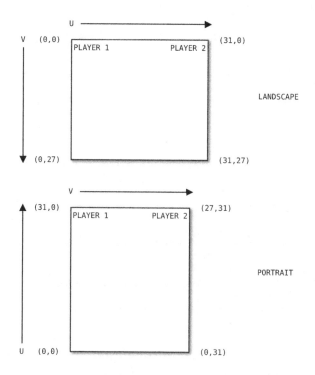

Figure 6.2: VIC Dual Video Layout

The layout of the cell grid is simple — rows and columns of bytes, each byte telling the video generator which of the 256 characters to use.

> Since many games have their monitors rotated 90 degrees in either direction, talking about coordinates gets confusing.
>
> In this book, we refer to X and Y as the horizontal and vertical coordinates, independent of monitor rotation.
>
> When we use the U coordinate, it means going in the direction of the electron beam, along a scanline. When we use V, it means across scanlines, perpendicular to U.
>
> If the monitor is in landscape mode then U is horizontal, and V is vertical. In portrait mode (rotated) U is vertical and V is horizontal.

6. THE VIC DUAL HARDWARE

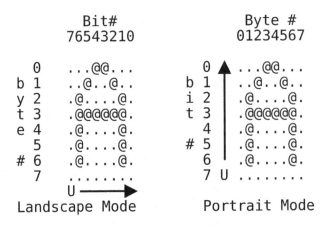

Figure 6.3: VIC Dual Tile Layout

---

array-type array-name[dimension1][dimension2]...

Declares an array of one or more dimensions.

We can also define a memory region using the __at keyword. It can be declared in C with a two-dimensional array at address $E000, 28 rows with 32 bytes each:

```
byte __at (0xe000) cellram[28][32];
```

($8000 or any of the other mirrored addresses would also work)

Note that C performs no bounds-checking, so the compiler will gleefully allow you to write outside of the array, and probably corrupt your variables in RAM and whatever else is in memory.

The 8x8 bitmaps for each character (tile) are declared as a different 2D array at address $E800:

```
byte __at (0xe800) tileram[256][8];
```

The ability to change the tile bitmaps in RAM makes for interesting possibilities, but it also means we have to initialize tile RAM before we see anything. First, we define our tile graphics in a C array:

```
const byte font8x8[0x100][8] = {
{ 0x00,0x00,0x00,0x00,0x00,0x00,0x00,0x00 }, { 0x7e,0x81, ...
};
```

If we multiply both dimensions of this array, we get $100 * 8 = $800 bytes. It's the same size as the tile RAM space, which is what we want.

Note that we we defined the `font8x8` array with the `const` keyword, to tell the compiler to store it in ROM. If we omit const, it'll be stored twice — once in ROM, and once in RAM, wasting space (more space than we have!)

> *sizeof(expr)*
>
> Returns the size of an expression in bytes.

At the start of the program, we copy the tile graphics from ROM to RAM with a call to the `memcpy` function:

```
memcpy(tileram, font8x8, sizeof(font8x8));
```

The `memcpy` takes three arguments: the destination pointer, the source pointer, and the number of bytes to copy. (Gack, what are "pointers"? Don't worry, we'll explain later.)

6.4 Colors

The VIC Dual introduces the concept of a *color palette*. A palette defines a mapping from values to colors.

In the VIC Dual, each palette has eight entries, each entry defining a background and foreground color for the cell. There are also only eight possible colors:

6. The VIC Dual Hardware

#	Bits	Color
0	...	Black
1	..R	Red
2	.G.	Green
3	.GR	Yellow
4	B..	Blue
5	B.R	Magenta
6	BG.	Cyan
7	BGR	White

To decide which entry of the palette is used for a given cell, the video generator looks at the upper three bits of the value in that cell. This gives us eight different byte ranges which correspond to eight colors:

Start	End	Palette Index
$00	$1F	0
$20	$3F	1
$40	$5F	2
$60	$7F	3
$80	$9F	4
$A0	$BF	5
$C0	$DF	6
$E0	$FF	7

Unfortunately, this means that each tile is locked to a particular palette entry. Later systems will let us assign different palettes to individual cells, but this design is relatively primitive.

This system has a total of four palettes, and to change to a different palette you can write to I/O port $40:

```
__sfr __at (0x40) palette; // I/O port $40
```

We've used two keywords here, __sfr which indicates a I/O port, and __at which defines the I/O address (in this case, 0x40).

You can write to the palette port like any other variable:

```
palette = 1; // set palette 1
```

The palette switch takes place immediately; the video generator uses the new palette from that point forward. This can be used for cool "lightning" effects that flash the screen.

The palette data is contained in a 32-byte *PROM* (Programmable Read-Only Memory) which we've mapped in our emulator ROM to address $4000. An example:

```
#define PE(fg,bg) (((fg)<<5) | ((bg)<<1))

const byte __at (0x4000) color_prom[32] = {
PE(7,0),PE(3,0),PE(1,0),PE(3,0),PE(6,0),PE(3,0),PE(2,0),PE(6,0),
PE(1,0),PE(2,0),PE(3,0),PE(4,0),PE(5,0),PE(6,0),PE(7,0),PE(0,7),
PE(7,0),PE(7,0),PE(7,0),PE(7,0),PE(3,0),PE(3,0),PE(3,0),PE(3,0),
PE(7,0),PE(7,0),PE(7,0),PE(7,0),PE(7,0),PE(7,0),PE(7,0),PE(7,0),
};
```

Each palette entry contains the foreground color in bits 5-7, and the background color in bits 1-3. To help us put the bits in the right places, we defined a preprocessor macro PE(fg,bg) that builds each palette entry at compile time.

(That macro is tricky, but you may have seen | (bitwise or) in a previous chapter. << means "shift left" — we'll cover that in a later chapter.)

6.5 Typedefs

> *typedef type name;*
>
> Defines *name* as an alias for the type definition *type*.

All C compilers have built-in *primitive types* to represent integers. The char type is usually 8 bits wide, but the other types vary depending on compiler.

6. The VIC Dual Hardware

Our compiler has the types described in the following table:

C type	Alias	Bits	Min. value	Max. value
unsigned char	byte	8	0	255
signed char	sbyte	8	-128	127
unsigned int	word	16	0	65535
int, short	-	16	-32768	32767
long	-	32	-2147483648	2147483647
float	-	32	-10^{38}	10^{38}

The `typedef` keyword defines a synonym (or alias) for a type, so you don't have to spell out the entire type declaration each time you use it. Typing `signed` and `unsigned` is a bit unwieldly, so in most of our sample programs, we use `typedef` statements to make aliases for types we use often:

```
typedef unsigned char byte;    // byte = 8 bits unsigned
typedef signed char sbyte;     // byte = 8 bits signed
typedef unsigned short word;   // word = 16 bits unsigned
typedef enum { false, true } bool; // boolean type (0 or 1)
```

The type definition comes first, then the identifier. For example, `byte` becomes an alias for `unsigned char`. (We'll discuss `enum` in the next chapter, but suffice to say it defines false = 0 and true = 1.)

6.6 A Minimal Main Function

 To see it on 8bitworkshop.com: Select the **VIC Dual** platform, then select the **Minimal Main** file.

This example `main` function does the following:

1. Sets the palette index to 1
2. Fills tile RAM with `$FE` bytes (binary `%11111110`)
3. Loops through all X and Y coordinates from 0 to 31, setting a different color for each row.
4. Goes into an infinite loop (stops the program.)

6.6. A Minimal Main Function

We start by declaring two 8-bit *local variables*, x and y (local variables must be declared at the beginning of a function):

```
void main() {
  byte x,y;
```

Then we set the palette index. Our palette is configured so that palette 1 gives us the full range of 8 colors:

```
  palette = 1;
```

Now we set up the tile RAM area which defines the bitmaps for each character. Normally we'd copy a predefined set of bitmaps to this area, but this is just a test, so we'll fill all the memory with the same byte.

We could fill up memory by writing a loop, but our C compiler's *standard library* has some nifty functions that manipulate blocks of memory. We'll use the memset function for this:

```
  memset(tileram, 0xfe, sizeof(tileram));
```

This just sets each byte in the tileram array to $FE. On the screen, this makes each tile look like a rectangular block.

---

array[i]

Indexes the ith element of *array*, with 0 being the first element.

We also want to fill the cellram memory, but it'll be boring if it's all the same byte. So we'll do it a different way, using the for statement. We loop through all the cells of the 32x32 buffer with two nested for loops:

```
  for (y=0; y<32; y++) {
    for (x=0; x<32; x++) {
      cellram[x][y] = y*8;
    }
  }
```

6. The VIC Dual Hardware

These two nested loops iterate over every combination of x and y from 0 to 31. First y=0 and the x values from 0 to 31, then y=1, etc. The cellram[x][y] syntax sets the appropriate byte in video RAM to the value on the right side of the =.

The loop fills each row with successive multiples of 8, from 0 all the way to 248. Since the color of a cell is determined by the upper 3 bits, we should see all 8 colors of the palette.

We don't have anything else to do, so we just go into an infinite loop. This is pretty easy with a `while` statement:

```
while (1) ;
```

The semicolon here denotes an *empty statement* (you could have also used an empty { } block.)

6.7 C Routines

If we don't want to deal with the `cellram` array directly, we can write some basic C functions that read and write particular cells:

```
void putchar(byte x, byte y, byte value) {
  cellram[x][y] = value;
}
byte getchar(byte x, byte y) {
  return cellram[x][y];
}
```

Or one that clears the entire screen, using the efficient library routine `memset`:

```
void clrscr() {
  memset(cellram, 0, sizeof(cellram));
}
```

Writing a string of characters to the screen is easy, too:

```
void putstring(byte x, byte y, const char* string) {
  while (*string) {
    putchar(x++, y, *string++);
  }
}
```

This function loops through the characters in the string until it hits a 0, which marks the end of the string. It calls `putchar` and increments the X position for each character. (The `string` parameter is a pointer — we'll talk about them soon!)

6.8 Controllers

The controller scheme differs between VIC Dual games, but we've chosen one for our emulator based on *Carnival*. It features a single left-right joystick and button; we've also added the up and down directions.

The controller inputs come in through the CPU's I/O ports; this game uses four of them:

```
__sfr __at (0x0) input0;
__sfr __at (0x1) input1;
__sfr __at (0x2) input2;
__sfr __at (0x3) input3;
```

When a switch is closed (i.e., button pushed or joystick moved) a particular bit in a particular input port changes state. "Active high" means that closing a switch (moving a joystick) changes the bit from 0 to 1, "active low" means it goes from 1 to 0.

We can test these switches using the bitwise AND operator ("&"). We combine a controller input with a *bitmask*, which has just a single bit set — the bit we wish to test. If the controller input also has this bit set, the AND operation will be non-zero, thus true (C considers all non-zero values to be "true"). Here we use binary notation for the bitmask value:

```
if (input1 & 0b00010000) { /* move left */ }
```

6. The VIC Dual Hardware

It's often easier to just use hex notation for a single bit:

```
if (input1 & 0x10) { /* move left */ }
```

> !expr
>
> If *expr* evaluates to true, return 0. Otherwise, return 1.

All of the switches in *Carnival* are active low except for the coin detector, so we invert them using the *boolean inversion* operator:

```
if (!(input1 & 0x10)) { /* move left */ }
```

It's easy to write C preprocessor macros to write expressions for all of the joystick directions, buttons, and coin detector:

```
#define LEFT1  !(input1 & 0x10)
#define RIGHT1 !(input1 & 0x20)
#define UP1    !(input1 & 0x40)
#define DOWN1  !(input1 & 0x80)
#define FIRE1  !(input2 & 0x20)
#define COIN1   (input3 & 0x8)
#define START1 !(input2 & 0x10)
#define START2 !(input3 & 0x20)
```

Then we can just use them like this:

```
if (LEFT1) { /* move left */ }
```

The coin detector in VIC Dual games is a special and interesting case. It's connected to the CPU reset line, so that when a coin is detected, the CPU is also reset. Although this means the program must start over, memory is not cleared. We can take advantage of this fact to increment a `credits` variable right after the `main` function starts:

```
  if (COIN1) {   // coin detected?
    credits++;   // add a credit
  } else {
    test_ram();  // no coin, reset RAM
  }
```

If we don't detect a coin right after reset, we assume the machine has just been plugged in, so we clear all the RAM and go on with our initialization routine. (Most arcade machines had a diagnostic test routine on initial startup.)

6.9 Z80 Entry Routine

Typically a C program starts with a built-in entry routine (called crt0 on most systems) which sets up some registers and memory, then calls the main() function.

Our embedded Z80 system doesn't have a built-in entry function, so we have to write our own — we'll call it start:

```
void main(); // we define main() later

void start() {
__asm
        LD      SP,#0xE800  ; set up stack pointer
        DI                  ; disable interrupts
__endasm;
        main();
}
```

First, we've declared the main() function; we'll define it (fill it out) later. Then we define the start() function, which includes some *inline assembly*, bracketed by the __asm and __endasm keywords. This feature lets us mix assembly code with our C code. Here, it sets up the stack pointer to the end of general-purpose RAM ($e800) and disables interrupts, which are not used on the VIC Dual platform.

start() needs to be the very first function we define, because as our entry point it needs to start at address 0x0, which the CPU goes to after a reset. The last thing it does it call the main() function, which we'll define as the proper start of our program.

7

Siege Game

We're now going to write a full game for the VIC Dual platform. As our inspiration, we'll use one of its early successes, *Blockade*, a game that's been replicated many times over the years.

There will be two players that can move in one of four cardinal directions, with no stopping. Each player leaves a trail behind them, and the goal is to get the other player to hit your trail or their own trail. The player that survives scores a point, and the game continues until one player gets a certain number of points.

In the grand spirit of lazy naming, we'll just use our thesarus and call this game *Siege*. We'll first go over a simple version of the game, which lacks scoring and coin-detection.

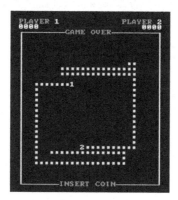

Figure 7.1: Our game for this chapter, "Siege"

7. Siege Game

 To see it on 8bitworkshop.com: Select the **VIC Dual** platform, then select the **Siege Game (prototype)** file.

7.1 Data Structures

When starting to program a game, we'll often think not only about what code to write, but which data structures best represent the state of the game world.

> ***struct** { field definitions ... }*
>
> Declares a struct type with the given field definitions.

For *Siege*, we need to track a lot of things for each player — their X and Y coordinate, direction of travel, etc. We use typedef to define a C *struct* type (called Player) that holds all of a player's attributes:

```
typedef struct {
  byte x;             // x coordinate
  byte y;             // y coordinate
  byte dir;           // direction (0-3)
  char head_attr;     // char to draw player
  char tail_attr;     // char to draw trail
  char collided;      // did we collide? 1 if so
} Player;
```

The typedef just defines a type, it does not declare a variable. So now that we have typedef'd our struct Player, we can declare an array to represent the two players.

```
Player players[2];    // two player structs
```

You can also define and declare structs in one step, without using a typedef:

```
struct {
  byte x;
  byte y;
  ...
} players[2];
```

It's usually better to use a `typedef`, though, because having the type around enables you to easily do things like declare pointers, which we'll make use of later.

> A note on C code style: We capitalize almost all user-defined types in this book, except for primitive types like `byte` and `word`. This helps us distinguish types from variables. The POSIX standard uses the `_t` suffix for its own types, but doesn't say anything about user-defined types. Anyway, let's assume it's 1978 and POSIX isn't even a thing yet.

7.2 Main Function

Now we go to the end of our program, where we define the `main` function:

```
void main() {
  palette = 0;
  memcpy(tileram, font8x8, sizeof(font8x8));
  draw_playfield();
  while (1) {
    init_game();
    play_round();
  }
}
```

(Why is the `main` function at the end? Because every function it calls has to be defined first, and so on for those functions.)

The first thing we do is set the video palette to 0, which gives us a nice yellow/cyan melange.

7. Siege Game

Figure 7.2: Code Page 437 font

Then we memcpy our bitmap data from or ROM array into the tile RAM. The 8x8 tiles are defined in a const array — 256 ($100) entries of 8 bytes each, like so:

```
const byte font8x8[0x100][8] = {
{ 0x00,0x00,0x00,0x00,0x00,0x00,0x00,0x00 }, // tile 0
{ 0x7e,0x81,0x95,0xb1,0xb1,0x95,0x81,0x7e }, // tile 1
...
};
```

The tile set we've chosen here is a classic 256-character font from the PC era, CP437 (Code Page 437) that contains lots of useful symbols – see Figure 7.2 for the full set.

Before we start the game, we set up the screen with draw_playfield – this just draws a border around the play area, which has its corners at (0,0) and (27,29):

```
void draw_playfield() {
  draw_box(0,0,27,29,BOX_CHARS);
}
```

> $--x$
> $++x$
>
> Increment or decrement x by 1.
>
> If this value is used in an expression, x is evaluated *after* the increment takes place.

7.2. Main Function

We also have to define `draw_box`:

```
const char BOX_CHARS[8] = { 218, 191, 192, 217, 196, 196, 179,
    179 };

void draw_box(byte x, byte y, byte x2, byte y2, const char
    chars[]) {
  byte x1 = x;
  // first draw the corners
  putchar(x, y, chars[2]);
  putchar(x2, y, chars[3]);
  putchar(x, y2, chars[0]);
  putchar(x2, y2, chars[1]);
  // draw the top/bottom sides
  while (++x < x2) {
    putchar(x, y, chars[5]);
    putchar(x, y2, chars[4]);
  }
  // draw the left/right sides
  while (++y < y2) {
    putchar(x1, y, chars[6]);
    putchar(x2, y, chars[7]);
  }
}
```

The `BOX_CHARS` array defines the 8 tile characters used for the corners and sides of the boxes. We've passed it as the `chars` parameter to `draw_box` so that you can make different kinds of boxes.

---
s.name

Indexes the field *name* of struct *s*.

The `init_game` function sets up the `Player` objects we defined earlier:

```
void init_game() {
  memset(players, 0, sizeof(players));
  players[0].head_attr = CHAR('1');
  players[1].head_attr = CHAR('2');
  players[0].tail_attr = 254;
  players[1].tail_attr = 254;
}
```

We use `memset` to fill the entire `players` array with zeroes, which is an easy way to set all the fields of the player objects to zero. Then we set the fields that we want to be non-zero, like the `head_attr` and `tail_attr` fields. Player 1's avatar will be a "1" and player 2 will be a "2." (Our game universe is very literal!)

We need a function to play a "round" of the game, which mean until one of the players hits something. We define `play_round`:

```
void play_round() {
  reset_players();
  clrscr();
  draw_playfield();
  while (1) { // loop indefinitely
    make_move();
    // exit loop if either player collided with something
    if (players[0].collided || players[1].collided) break;
  }
  flash_colliders();
}
```

Note the `while (1)` loop. The `while` keyword loops as long as its condition in parenthesis evaluates to true. Its condition is just 1, which means it'll loop forever. Fortunately, we have the `break` keyword, which immediately exits the current loop. So we exit the loop when either player collides with something:

```
if (players[0].collided || players[1].collided) break;
```

Now let's go through the `play_round` function. First, `reset_players` sets up the initial position of the two players at the start of the round, and the initial direction of movement:

```
void reset_players() {
  players[0].x = players[0].y = 6;
  players[0].dir = D_RIGHT;
  players[1].x = players[1].y = 21;
  players[1].dir = D_LEFT;
  players[0].collided = players[1].collided = 0;
}
```

We define the four cardinal directions using an `enum` typedef, which is a handy way of declaring constants:

7.2. Main Function

```
typedef enum { D_RIGHT, D_DOWN, D_LEFT, D_UP } Direction;
```

This effectively defines the following constants:

```
D_RIGHT = 0
D_DOWN  = 1
D_LEFT  = 2
D_UP    = 3
```

> C style note: Constant values and macro definitions are often declared in ALL_CAPS. Don't worry, we're not yelling at you!

The heart of the game is the `make_move` function:

```c
void make_move() {
  byte i;
  // delay and read control inputs
  for (i=0; i<FRAMES_PER_MOVE; i++) {
    human_control(0);
    wait_for_vsync();
  }
  // decide computer player's move
  ai_control(1);
  // move 2nd player
  move_player(1);
  // move 1st player
  move_player(0);
}
```

The `human_control` and `ai_control` functions determine which direction the players will go on their next move, while the `move_player` function moves them and checks for collisions.

Why do we loop `FRAMES_PER_MOVE` times? This is a delay loop that controls the speed of the game. Each iteration calls `wait_for_vsync` (described in the previous chapter) which waits until the start of a new frame. So each iteration pauses up to 1/60 second.

7. Siege Game

We also call human_control during the delay loop, because we want to detect control inputs that occur within this time. Checking every 0.0167 seconds should be frequent enough for even the quickest joystick-wrangler. The function is pretty simple:

```
void human_control(byte p) {
  Direction dir = 0xff;
  if (LEFT1) dir = D_LEFT;
  if (RIGHT1) dir = D_RIGHT;
  if (UP1) dir = D_UP;
  if (DOWN1) dir = D_DOWN;
  // don't let the player reverse
  if (dir != 0xff && dir != (players[p].dir ^ 2)) {
    players[p].dir = dir;
  }
}
```

We declare a local variable of type Direction, first setting it to $FF as a "no change" indicator (we can do this because enum types are treated like integer types by the compiler.) We then check each joystick directional input using the LEFT1/RIGHT1/UP1/DOWN1 macros we've previously defined.

We don't want the player to reverse direction, because then they would immediately hit their own trail. So if we're going left, we want to prevent the player from going right.

That's where the players[p].dir ^ 2 expression comes in. The ^ operator is a bitwise *exclusive-or* (XOR) which flips the bits of one operand based on the bits set in the other. Going back to our directional constants, let's look at them in binary and see how they respond to the XOR:

```
D_RIGHT = %00  ^  %10  =  %10
D_DOWN  = %01  ^  %10  =  %11
D_LEFT  = %10  ^  %10  =  %00
D_UP    = %11  ^  %10  =  %01
```

Flipping the second bit effectively gives us the reverse direction, which we can then check to make sure we don't go that way.

7.2. Main Function

The move_player function erases the player (replacing it with the trail character) and moves it one square in the current direction. We also want to check to see if the player collided with their own trail, or the other player's trail.

We're already drawing both trails to the screen, so we can just check video RAM! If anything but a blank character is in a player's space (we use the getchar function to check), we set the collided flag. Only then do we replace the player's current position with a trail character, and draw the player's head character in the new space.

```
void move_player(byte p) {
  erase_player(p);
  players[p].x += DIR_X[players[p].dir];
  players[p].y += DIR_Y[players[p].dir];
  if (getchar(players[p].x, players[p].y) != CHAR(' '))
    players[p].collided = 1;
  draw_player(p);
}
```

DIR_X and DIR_Y are lookup tables that help us convert a Direction value to a X and Y coordinate offset (note we use the signed char type, not byte, since values can be negative):

```
const char DIR_X[4] = { 1, 0, -1, 0 };
const char DIR_Y[4] = { 0, -1, 0, 1 };
```

The draw_player and erase_player just set the appropriate character tile at the player's position, and are pretty simple (though generate a surprising amount of code):

```
void draw_player(byte p) {
  putchar(players[p].x, players[p].y, players[p].head_attr);
}

void erase_player(byte p) {
  putchar(players[p].x, players[p].y, players[p].tail_attr);
}
```

We also have an AI player. It's very simple, almost simpler than the human player. The computer player just looks ahead one space, and turns to the right if anything is there other than a blank space:

```
void ai_control(byte p) {
  byte x,y;
  Direction dir = players[p].dir;
  x = players[p].x + DIR_X[dir];
  y = players[p].y + DIR_Y[dir];
  if (getchar(x,y) != CHAR(' ')) {
    players[p].dir = (dir + 1) & 3;
  }
}
```

The (dir + 1) & 3 expression turns to the right, since our directions are in clockwise order. The & is a bitwise AND operation — it only keeps the bits that are in both operands. In this context, it wraps the direction value to the range 0 to 3. This is often called a *bitmask*.

We want some kind of reaction from the game when a player collides, so flash_colliders will provide that:

```
void flash_colliders() {
  byte i;
  // flash players that collided
  for (i=0; i<60; i++) {
    if (players[0].collided) players[0].head_attr ^= 0x80;
    if (players[1].collided) players[1].head_attr ^= 0x80;
    wait_for_vsync();
    wait_for_vsync();
    draw_player(0);
    draw_player(1);
    palette = i;
  }
  palette = 0;
}
```

This function loops for a couple of seconds, cycling between different palettes. It also tweaks the character of the colliding player(s) to highlight who ran into something.

And that's it for the basic game! The full game on the 8bitworkshop website has several improvements: accepting virtual coins, an "attract mode," scoring, and a smarter AI player.

8

Shift and Rotate

8.1 Shift Operations

The Z80 has a good variety of shift and rotate instructions:

SLA	Shift Left	Shift left 1 bit, bit 7 → Carry
SRL	Shift Right (Logical)	Shift right 1 bit, bit 0 → Carry, 0 → bit 7
SRA	Shift Right (Arithmetic)	Shift right 1 bit, bit 0 → Carry, bit 7 unchanged
RL	Rotate Left	9-bit rotation, Carry → bit 0
RR	Rotate Right	9-bit rotation, Carry → bit 7
RLC	Rotate Left thru Carry	8-bit rotation, Carry → bit 0
RRC	Rotate Right thru Carry	8-bit rotation, Carry → bit 7
RLD	Rotate Left (D)	12-bit rotation, LSB=(HL), MSB=A
RRD	Rotate Right (D)	12-bit rotation, LSB=(HL), MSB=A

Table 8.1: Shift and rotate instructions

The "shift" instructions move bits one position left or right within a byte. The bit that is shifted off the edge of the byte (i.e. the high bit for shift left, and the low bit for shift right) gets put into the Carry flag.

The "rotate" instructions shift the previous Carry flag into the other end of the byte. So for rotate left, the Carry flag is copied into the rightmost (low) bit. For rotate right, it's copied into the leftmost (high) bit. The RL/RR instructions perform 9-bit rotation, using the Carry flag as the 9th bit. The RLC/RRC instructions perform 8-bit rotation, copying the shifted bit to the Carry flag.

8. Shift and Rotate

> *expr* << *n*
>
> In C, compute *expr* shifted left by *n* bits.

Let's say we wanted a function to double the player's score. We could accomplish this by shifting left by 1 bit:

```
void double_score() {
    score <<= 1;
}
```

Since score is a 16-bit variable, we need to first shift the low byte left, which moves its high bit into the Carry flag. Then we rotate the high byte left, shifting the Carry flag into its low bit:

```
_double_score::
        ld      iy,#_score
        sla     0 (iy)          ; left shift lo byte
        rl      1 (iy)          ; left shift hi byte w/ carry
        ret
```

The nn (IY) addressing mode computes the effective address as [IY + #nn], allowing us to address both bytes without explicitly incrementing IY.

8.1. Shift Operations

> *expr >> n*
>
> In C, compute *expr* shifted right by *n* bits. If *a* is signed, performs an arithmetic shift (fill high bits with 1s) otherwise a logical shift (fill high bits with 0s).

Cutting the score in half (score >> 1) involves a right shift and a right rotate, starting with the high byte of score:

```
_halve_score::
        ld      iy,#_score
        sra     1 (iy)          ; right shift hi byte
        rr      0 (iy)          ; right shift lo byte w/ carry
        ret
```

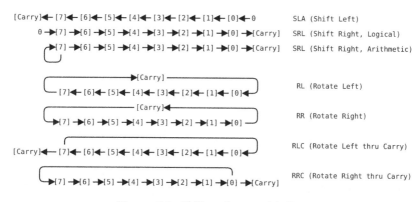

Figure 8.1: Shift and rotate bit flow

9
The Programmable Sound Generator

Video games have had sound since the first *Computer Space* debuted at a convention for jukeboxes. In early arcade game designs, the sound board was often custom-made for each title, and included a variety of sound circuits that could be triggered from the main CPU board. Since the sounds were hard-wired, there was usually little control except "start" and sometimes "stop."

Even after the mid-1970s when CPUs got cheap enough to be used in video games, designers still used discrete circuits for sound generation. These circuits often made use of the ubiquitous 555 timer chip to output a simple oscillating signal, sometimes modified by resistor-capacitor filters and/or envelopes. For example, Atari's *Pong* could generate three different sounds — bounce (a short 246 Hz pulse), score (a long 246 Hz pulse), and hit (a short 491 Hz pulse).[3]

As the market for video games and electronic gadgets grew, chipmakers developed integrated circuits that produced various sorts of noises in a single chip. One of the first was the Texas Instruments SN76477 "Complex Sound Generator," which could be described as a mostly-analog monophonic synthesizer.

The SN76477 was not programmable, but controlled by external capacitors and resistors, sometimes requiring other ICs for more complex noises. The data sheet describes example circuits

9. The Programmable Sound Generator

Figure 9.1: AY-3-8912 chip, 28-pin DIP package

such as "BIRD CHIRP," "STEAM TRAIN WITH WHISTLE," and "RACE CAR MOTOR/CRASH." In the post 8-bit era, this chip is beloved by DIY synthesizer tinkerers, and it had a production run as recently as 2008.

As microprocessors got cheaper and the personal computer revolution began in earnest, it was clear that noisemakers should be controlled by software, not by hard-coded circuits. Programmable sound generator (PSG) chips would fulfill this function, producing a variety of sounds with no additional components required. The output was determined exclusively by a set of registers which were programmed by a CPU.

9.1 The AY-3-8910 PSG

The General Instrument AY-3-8910 is an popular PSG designed in 1978. It was intended to be paired with the company's CP1600 CPU (used by the Intellivision console) but it and its variants were used in many arcade games, pinball machines, game consoles, and home computers over the next decade and beyond. In fact, as of 2010 there were still slot machines being produced with compatible sound chips!

The AY-3-8910 PSG has three primary voices (tone generators) and one noise channel. Each voice can emit a tone chosen from 4095 different pitches by dividing a base frequency by a 12-bit value. The noise source can be set to one of 32 different periods (frequencies).

The 8910 has 16 8-bit registers that control its output. (Some bits of some registers are unused, and some registers control the GPIO ports which we won't cover here.)

9.1. The AY-3-8910 PSG

Reg #	Bits 76543210	Description
R0	XXXXXXXX	Channel A Tone Period (Low)
R1	XXXX	Channel A Tone Period (High)
R2	XXXXXXXX	Channel B Tone Period (Low)
R3	XXXX	Channel B Tone Period (High)
R4	XXXXXXXX	Channel C Tone Period (Low)
R5	XXXX	Channel C Tone Period (High)
R6	...XXXXX	Noise Period Control
R7	.....BCA ..BCA...	Channel Enable (Tone) 1=off Channel Enable (Noise) 1=off
R8	...EVVVV	Channel A Env Enable, Volume
R9	...EVVVV	Channel B Env Enable, Volume
R10	...EVVVV	Channel C Env Enable, Volume
R11	XXXXXXXX	Envelope Period (Low Byte)
R12	XXXX	Envelope Period (High Byte)
R13	....CALH	Envelope Shape (Continue, Attack, Alternate, Hold)

Figure 9.2: AY-3-8910 Registers

Programming the AY-3-8910 typically involves two steps: select a register, then set the value. For example, on the VIC Dual platform we've connected the chip so that port 1 selects the register and port 2 sets the value. Using the __sfr keyword, we can define these two ports in C:

```
__sfr __at (0x1) ay8910_reg;
__sfr __at (0x2) ay8910_data;
```

We can also define a convenience function to set the value of a specific register:

```
inline void set8910(byte reg, byte data) {
  ay8910_reg = reg;
  ay8910_data = data;
}
```

To demonstrate, let's create a function to play a tone on one of the three channels:

67

9. The Programmable Sound Generator

```
inline void play_tone(byte channel, word period, byte volume)
```

To play a tone on one of the three channels, first set the Low/High Tone Period registers to choose the desired frequency. A channel's tone frequency is defined by this equation:

$$Frequency = \frac{Clock}{16 * TonePeriod}$$

In most designs, the clock frequency is 3.579545 Mhz. A period of 0 is invalid (the data sheet doesn't even say what'll happen, but people knew not to divide by zero in those days!)

You can also rearrange the equation thusly:

$$TonePeriod = \frac{Clock}{16 * Frequency}$$

Using our set8910 function, the Tone Period registers can be set like this (assuming period is a 16-bit variable):

```
set8910(channel*2+0, period & 0xff); // lo byte
set8910(channel*2+1, period >> 8);   // hi byte
```

Then set the Channel Volume register, which ranges from 0 to 15 (4 bits):

```
set8910(channel+8, volume); // set volume
```

Now enable the channel by clearing its corresponding bit in the Channel Enable register:

```
set8910(7, ~(1<<channel)); // enable tone
```

~x

Invert all bits in x.

9.1. The AY-3-8910 PSG

To turn off the channel, just set the bit in the Channel Enable register:

```
set8910(7, 1<<channel); // disable tone
```

If you plan to use multiple channels, you should track the Channel Enable bits in a variable, and set or clear them as neccessary before updating the register.

Playing noise is similar, but there is only one Noise Period register which defines the upper frequency of noise – higher values produce lower frequencies:

$$NoiseUpperFrequency = \frac{Clock}{16 * Period}$$

The noise generator can be mixed into any of the three channels, whether a tone is playing or not. This example sets the Noise Period register, the Channel Volume, and enables the noise bit in the Channel Enable register:

```
set8910(6, noise_period); // set noise period
set8910(channel+8, volume); // set volume
set8910(7, ~(8<<channel)); // enable noise
```

These operations can be performed in any order, but note that on the actual hardware, the register changes take effect instantly, and there will be some CPU delay between register changes.

The 8910 also has an envelope generator, but this is rarely used as it must be shared among all three channels (and our emulator doesn't support it as of this writing). For more information, you can check out the original General Instrument datasheet.[4]

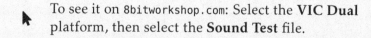
To see it on 8bitworkshop.com: Select the **VIC Dual** platform, then select the **Sound Test** file.

9. THE PROGRAMMABLE SOUND GENERATOR

9.2 Inline Functions

Since the `set8910()` function is pretty simple, we defined it with the `inline` keyword. This forces the compiler to expand it in-place instead of performing a function call. In some cases, this not only saves CPU cycles, but code space as well.

For comparison, this is the assembly output without the `inline` keyword:

```
0912 21 07 08      [10] 2326      ld      hl, #0x0807
0915 E3            [19] 2327      ex      (sp),hl
0916 CD 7E 08      [17] 2328      call    _set8910
```

And here it is with `inline`:

```
08FF 3E 07         [ 7] 2309      ld      a,#0x07
0901 D3 01         [11] 2310      out     (_ay8910_reg),a
0903 3E 08         [ 7] 2312      ld      a,#0x08
0905 D3 02         [11] 2313      out     (_ay8910_data),a
```

The `inline` version takes just one extra byte of code per call, but saves at least 10 CPU cycles per call (plus 50+ cycles for the `set8910()` function itself.) Also, when using `inline`, the function itself won't be compiled, which saves even more ROM space.

Inline functions also take advantage of *constant folding*. If all variables in an expression like `channel*2+1` are constants, the compiler will evaluate it at compile-time, saving many CPU instructions. Constant folding is performed when inlining, so any constants passed to the function will likely be optimized.

In this case, using `inline` was a win. You can easily check to see if using `inline` improves your code by comparing the size of your ROM with and without it. Short and simple functions tend to do well with inlining.

10

Binary-Coded Decimal

Up to this point, we've only dealt with bytes encoded in binary — which represent unsigned values from 0 to 255. Now we're going to use *binary-coded decimal* or *BCD* values.

BCD represents numbers in a more human-readable format. Bytes are split in half, into two 4-bit "nibbles," which each contain a decimal digit from 0 to 9. In this scheme, the hexadecimal value reads the same as the decimal representation. For example, $00 to $09 are the same, but 10 is stored as $10, 11 is $11, etc. all the way up to $99.

Some early computers used the BCD representation for their number-crunching, and mainframes used them for processing financial data. They are still handy in the 8-bit world, foremost because they are easier to render to the screen. We don't have to divide by 10 to convert them to decimal digits, because the decimal digits are already part of the representation.

To extract the two digits from a BCD byte, we just shift by 4 to isolate the first digit (the high nibble) and mask by binary second digit (the low nibble):

```
void bcd2digits(byte bcd) {
  char digit1 = '0' + (bcd >> 4);
  char digit2 = '0' + (bcd & 0xf);
  ...
}
```

In C, we might find it handy to operate with 16-bit BCD numbers, which hold a total of 4 decimal digits. Here's a

10. BINARY-CODED DECIMAL

function to render all 4 digits to a given X/Y position on the screen, by shifting and masking each successive digit:

```
void draw_bcd_word(byte x, byte y, word bcd) {
  byte j;
  x += 3;
  for (j=0; j<4; j++) {
    putchar(x, y, CHAR('0'+(bcd & 0xf)));
    x--;
    bcd >>= 4;
  }
}
```

We can write a BCD addition routine in straight C, but a more efficient way would be to use the Z80's DAA instruction – it takes the result of an standard binary addition and converts it into a BCD result. The final function looks like this:

```
word bcd_add(word a, word b) __naked {
  a; b; // to avoid compiler warning
  __asm
          push    ix
          ld      ix,#0
          add     ix,sp
          ld      a,4 (ix)      ; load low byte
          add     a, 6 (ix)     ; add w/o carry
          daa                   ; correct to BCD
          ld      c,a
          ld      a,5 (ix)      ; load high byte
          adc     a, 7 (ix)     ; add w/ carry
          daa                   ; correct to BCD
          ld      b,a
          ld      l, c
          ld      h, b          ; store result in HL
          pop     ix
          ret
  __endasm;
}
```

(How this code was written: Write the C code for a simple 16-bit addition function, take the assembled output, and add a DAA instruction after the two ADD and ADC instructions. I love it when a plan comes together!)

11

Pointers

Earlier we promised to talk about pointers, and so here we are! So what is a *pointer*? That question has an simple answer, but to really understand them you have to see them at work. So let's start:

11.1 A Pointer is a Typed Memory Address

A pointer is just a memory location with a type attached. Internally, it's a 16-bit number, since the Z80 uses 16-bit addresses.

> *type* * *name*
>
> Declares a pointer that points to an object of type *type*.

We declare a pointer by putting a * after the type. So a pointer to a byte named ptr would be declared like this:

```
byte* ptr;
```

You can assign pointers just like you would any other variable — they're just 16-bit values underneath. In fact, you can directly set them to a memory address:

```
byte* ptr = (byte*)0x4800;
```

The (byte*) is a *type cast* which converts the number to a pointer.

11. Pointers

11.2 A Pointer is a Reference To Another Variable

Usually, you don't want to set the address of a pointer directly, but you want to set it to the address of another variable. You can create a pointer to any object using the & operator.

> &*x*
>
> Returns a pointer to *x*.

In this example, we first set x to 10. We then declare a pointer and set it to the address of x. Then through the pointer, we set x to 20:

```
byte x = 10;
byte* ptr = &x;
*ptr = 20;
```

Note the last line, *ptr = 20. The * means we're *dereferencing* the pointer — in other words, we're no longer treating it as a pointer, but as the object at the other end of the pointer.

> **x
>
> Dereferences the pointer *x* (reverses the & operator.)

Pointers are especially useful when dealing with arrays, because you can compute a pointer to a particular array index once, using it for multiple operations.

11.3 A Pointer is a String

In our "Hello World" chapter, we printed a string:

```
printf("HELLO WORLD"); // output some text
```

What we actually passed to the printf function, though, was a pointer. We could have rewritten the code like this:

```
char* text = "HELLO WORLD"; // pointer to string
printf(text);
```

In C, a string is just a pointer to an array of char, usually terminated by a zero byte (or *null terminator*.) We could have also rewritten our code like this:

```
char text[12] =
  {'H','E','L','L','O',' ','W','O','R','L','D',0};
printf(text);
```

Wait a second, doesn't text[12] define an array? How are we passing it to printf, which takes a pointer argument? The C compiler will convert the array to a pointer, passing the address of the first element of the array.

11.4 A Pointer is an Array ... Sort Of

Pointers and arrays have a lot in common, and often can be used interchangeably. For example, this function draws a string to the screen one character at a time:

```
void putstring(byte x, byte y, const char* string) {
  byte i;
  for (i=0; string[i]; i++) {
    putchar(x++, y, string[i]);
  }
}
```

Note the for statement where we use string[i] as the condition. This makes the loop continue as long as the current character is non-zero; i.e. we exit when we hit the final zero byte.

We can rewrite this function using pointers exclusively:

```
void putstring(byte x, byte y, const char* string) {
  while (*string) {
    putchar(x++, y, *string++);
  }
}
```

11. Pointers

We've seen the ++ operator before, when incrementing an integer by 1. But since string is a pointer type, can you add a number to a pointer? You can — this is called *pointer arithmetic*.

When incrementing (or adding or subtracting) pointers, you multiply by the size of the element to which it is pointing, based on the pointer's type. This makes it easy to iterate through arrays of multi-byte objects. For this example, string points to a char type, so the pointer will increment by 1.

The expression *char++ is a combination of the * and ++ operators. For clarity, we could rewrite it like this:

```
putchar(x, y, *string);
x++;
string++;
```

> Note that we put the keyword const before the pointer declaration byte* string. This means the data addressed by the pointer cannot be changed by the function. The compiler will give a warning if you try to modify the pointer's data, or if you try to convert the pointer to a non-const parameter.

11.5 A Pointer is an Extra Return Value

Pointers are nice for passing into functions, but we can use them to get data *out* of functions as well. Let's say we had a function that we wanted to return more than one value:

void get_hit_point(**int*** x, **int*** y)

Here we pass the pointers x and y into the function. Since they're pointers, we can use them not only as inputs (if we want to) but also as outputs.

12

The Midway 8080 Hardware

12.1 History

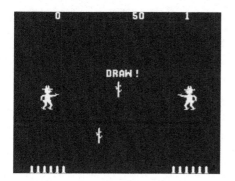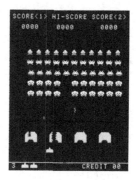

Figure 12.1: Midway's "Gun Fight" (left) and Taito's "Space Invaders" (right)

The first arcade game to use a microprocessor was *Gun Fight*. Taito originally designed the Japanese version with discrete circuits. Dave Nutting adapted the U.S. version for Midway, and chose to base it on the Intel 8080 CPU which he had used in pinball projects.[5] The original designer, Tomohiro Nishikado, was intrigued by the design and would later go on to create *Space Invaders* using a similar architecture.[6]

The Midway 8080 architecture generates video from a black-and-white *frame buffer*, using a whopping 7KB of RAM. (In 1975, the production run of *Gun Fight* used $3 million worth of RAM, estimated to be 60 percent of the world's supply.[7])

12.2 Memory Map

Start	End	Description
$0000	$1FFF	ROM
$2000	$23FF	General-purpose RAM
$2400	$3FFF	Video frame buffer RAM

Table 12.1: Midway 8080 Memory Map

> The Z80 runs Intel 8080 code unmodified; so, in the 8bitworkshop emulator we just use a simulated Z80.

12.3 Graphics

The video frame has 256 horizontal by 224 vertical pixels, and also can be rotated 90 degrees, as it is in *Space Invaders*. Each byte corresponds to eight pixels – for each bit, 1 means a lit pixel, 0 means dark. There are 32 bytes per scanline, thus 32 * 8 = 256 pixels across (or upwards if the screen is rotated.)

Since the Midway 8080 doesn't have any dedicated sprite hardware, we have to write code to draw and erase sprites in frame buffer RAM.

The most basic method we can implement to draw a sprite is to simply copy bytes from a bitmap to a rectangle on the screen. We'll have an outer loop that iterates through the scanlines of the sprite, and an inner loop that copies bytes to the screen.

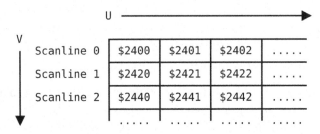

Figure 12.2: Midway 8080 frame buffer layout

12.3. Graphics

 To see it on 8bitworkshop.com: Select the **Midway 8080** platform, then select the **Graphics Test** file.

The screen memory is defined with a 224x32 byte array:

`byte __at (0x2400) vidmem[224][32]; // 256x224x1 video memory`

One of the most basic things we'd want to do is draw a sprite, or bitmap, to the screen. We'll write a `draw_sprite` function:

`void draw_sprite(const byte* src, byte x, byte y)`

It takes three parameters, the first of which is a *pointer* to the sprite data:

- src - pointer to sprite definition/bitmap
- x - starting cross-scan (V) coordinate
- y - starting scanwise (U) coordinate

Our sprite definition starts with two bytes giving the width and height of the sprite, followed by the bitmap data, e.g.:

```
const byte tiny_2x16_bitmap[] = {
 2, 2,
 0x88,0x88,0x44,0x44};
```

(The width is given in bytes, so multiply it by 8 to get pixels. Our screen is rotated, so the width is actually the height.)

To draw the sprite, we first compute a pointer to the corner of the target rectangle in video memory:

```
byte i,j;
byte* dest = &vidmem[x][y]; // get pointer to destination
```

Using the `src` pointer, we then fetch the width and height of the sprite, found in the first and second bytes of the sprite definition:

```
byte w = *src++;       // fetch width, advance src
byte h = *src++;       // fetch height, advance src
```

12. The Midway 8080 Hardware

The `src` pointer should now point to the bitmap data, which follows immediately after the width and height bytes. We now loop through the bitmap data, copying it to the screen:

```
for (j=0; j<h; j++) {
  for (i=0; i<w; i++) {
    *dest++ = *src++;
  }
  dest += 32-w;
}
```

At the end of the inner loop, we'll have copied all the bytes for the current scanline. We then add $32 - w$ to the `dest` pointer, which moves us to the next scanline (we've already copied w bytes, so we subtract it from 32, the byte length of a scanline.)

Note that our sprite functions perform no *clipping* – that is, they do not check to see if the sprite boundaries go beyond the video frame, and doing so will overwrite parts of memory outside of the frame buffer.

12.4 Draw vs. Erase vs. XOR

With a slight variation, we can also erase the sprites — just replace the inner loop with this expression:

```
*dest++ = 0;
```

Instead of copying bytes from the bitmap, we just set them all to 0.

One problem with the draw/erase method thus far is that it leaves an ugly black rectangle around all of our sprites. Each sprite will overwrite anything that has previously been drawn, including other sprites and the background.

One solution for this is to draw with XOR (exclusive-or). As we briefly covered in Chapter 2, XOR is a bit operation that combines the source and destination pixels according to these rules:

12.4. Draw vs. Erase vs. XOR

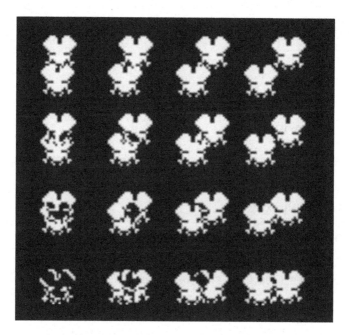

Figure 12.3: Overlapping sprites drawn with XOR

Source	Destination	Result
0	0	0
1	0	1
0	1	1
1	1	0

The first nifty property of XOR is that it won't obliterate everything in the target rectangle. Drawing blank pixels will leave existing pixels alone.

The second nifty property is that drawing the same thing with XOR twice completely erases the thing, restoring whatever it may have obscured. So you really only need one function to both draw and erase sprites.

The drawback to this method is that if you do overlap one object with another, any white pixels in both objects will become black pixels. This is the price you pay for reversibility.

Changing our routine to use XOR is simple, just use the ^ operator:

```
*dest++ ^= *src++;
```

12.5 Drawing Text

Text is very similar to sprites; we just keep the font bitmap in a two-dimensional array, like this:

```
#define LOCHAR 0x20
#define HICHAR 0x5e
#define CHAR(ch) ((ch)-LOCHAR)

const byte font8x8[HICHAR-LOCHAR+1][8] = {
  { 0x00,0x00,0x00,0x00,0x00,0x00,0x00,0x00 }, { 0x00,0x00, ...
}
```

The macro LOCHAR defines the first character in the font array, here set to 32 — which is where printable characters start (32 == Space). It's up to the programmer to only use characters between LOCHAR and HICHAR. The CHAR macro converts a character to a font index by subtracting LOCHAR.

The draw_char function looks very much like the sprite functions, except we have a hard-coded width and height, and we multiply x by 8 to simulate a grid of character cells:

```
void draw_char(char ch, byte x, byte y) {
  byte i;
  byte* dest = &vidmem[x*8][y];
  const byte* src = &font8x8[CHAR(ch)][0];
  for (i=0; i<8; i++) {
    *dest ^= *src;
    dest += 32;
    src += 1;
  }
}
```

12.6 Pixel-Accurate Sprite Shifting

The Midway 8080 boards also included a chip, the Fujitsu MB14241, which could arguably be called the first *GPU* (Graphics Processor Unit) included in a video game.

Its operation was quite simple: It had an internal 16-bit register that the CPU could set, and it would return a shifted 8-bit quantity at any bit offset within that register. Since the 8080 didn't have a barrel shifter (i.e., it could only shift by one bit per instruction) this would allow sprites to be easily drawn at any X coordinate, not just at 8 pixel intervals. Not all games used the chip, however.

Every time the `bitshift_value` register is written, the 16-bit register is shifted right by 8 bits, making room for the new byte which is put in the upper 8 bits:

```
XXXXXXXXYYYYYYYY
------->
new byte
        old byte
```

Reading from `bitshift_read` returns an 8-bit window of this 16-bit register, shifted by the number of bits set in the `bitshift_offset` register:

```
XXXXXXXXYYYYYYYY
   <------>         offset = 5
new byte
        old byte
```

The variables are declared as I/O ports using `__sfr`:

```
__sfr __at (0x2) bitshift_offset;
__sfr __at (0x4) bitshift_value;
volatile __sfr __at (0x3) bitshift_read;
```

The *volatile* keyword tells the C optimizer that a variable may change unexpectedly, and not to assume that a previous value that was read can be reused in later expressions. Since `bitshift_read` changes as a result of a write to `bitshift_value`, it needs the volatile keyword. (In the SDCC compiler, using the __at keyword seems to imply volatile, but we're trying to create good habits here!)

Given all that, here is a function to use the MB14241 to draw a shifted version of a sprite at an exact X and Y coordinate.

```
void draw_shifted_sprite(const byte* src, byte x, byte y) {
  byte i,j;
  byte* dest = &vidmem[x][y>>3];
  byte w = *src++;
  byte h = *src++;
  bitshift_offset = y & 7;       // set shift amount (0-7)
  for (j=0; j<h; j++) {
    bitshift_value = 0;          // write zero padding
    for (i=0; i<w; i++) {
      bitshift_value = *src++;   // write next sprite byte
      *dest++ = bitshift_read;   // read next shifted byte
    }
    bitshift_value = 0;          // write zero padding
    *dest++ = bitshift_read;     // read last shifted byte
    dest += 31-w;
  }
}
```

Note that we use zero padding both before and after writing a line of the sprite. If our background was white, we'd write a 0xff instead.

 To see it on 8bitworkshop.com: Select the **Midway 8080** platform, then select the **Sprite w/ Bit Shifter** file.

12.7 Watchdog Timer

The *watchdog* is an internal timer that tries to prevent errant code or faulty hardware from hanging up the game. Your program must "pet the dog" every so often – if you don't, the dog gets scared because it thinks your code went into an infinite loop. The dog is unhappy because your arcade game won't accept any more quarters! The dog barks, which resets your CPU – probably also ending the current game. So you should make sure to keep the dog happy!

The Midway 8080 watchdog lives at I/O port 6, and can be pet by writing any value. If you don't, it'll reset the CPU after 1.1 seconds. Here we show you how to make a `WATCHDOG` macro which does this:

```
__sfr __at (0x6) watchdog_strobe;

#define WATCHDOG watchdog_strobe = 0; // reset watchdog
```

13

Game: Cosmic Impalas

Now that we understand the Midway 8080 hardware a little bit, we're going to create a little game called "Cosmic Impalas." You control a little ship at the bottom of the screen and shoot at meanies that descend from above.

> To see it on 8bitworkshop.com: Select the **Midway 8080** platform, then select the **Cosmic Impalas** file.

13.1 Game Data

First, we have a bunch of global variables for bookkeeping:

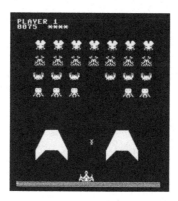

Figure 13.1: Our game for this chapter, "Cosmic Impalas"

13. Game: Cosmic Impalas

```
byte attract;      // in attract mode? 0 = no, 1 = yes
byte credits;      // number of coins inserted
byte curplayer;    // current player index (0 or 1)

word score;        // current score
byte lives;        // current # of lives

#define MAXLIVES 5     // maximum # of lives displayed
```

We have only one player object (the player's ship) and it is always at the same Y position, so we just have to track its X position. We decide it's sufficient to only have one bullet (from the player) and bomb (from an enemy) at a time, so we make their positions global variables as well:

```
byte player_x;     // player X position (0xff = gone)
byte bullet_x;     // player bullet X
byte bullet_y;     // player bullet Y (0 = gone)
byte bomb_x;       // enemy bomb X
byte bomb_y;       // enemy bomb Y (0 = gone)
```

Now, we will define an enemy ship with the `Enemy` struct, giving it a position and a sprite bitmap:

```
typedef struct {
  byte x,y;              // X, Y position
  const byte* shape;     // pointer to sprite shape
} Enemy;
```

C doesn't have any built-in *data structures* like variable-size lists, so you usually have to build your own or use a library. Here we use a fixed-size array to simulate a resizable list. We'll store the enemy ships in an array with 28 slots, to allow for a 7 x 4 formation:

```
#define MAX_ENEMIES 28

Entity entities[MAX_ENEMIES];    // array of enemies
byte num_entities;               // current # of enemies
```

Whenever an enemy is destroyed, we'll decrement `num_entities` and move the array slots in memory to fill in the gap left by the deleted object.

Updating all of the enemies in formation every frame would be difficult, so we'll just update one per frame. The variable entity_index keeps track of which entity is being updated:

`byte enemy_index;`

> *type name:N;*
>
> Defines a *bit field*; a type that only takes up *N* bits in the struct.
>
> Bit fields usually require extra CPU instructions to decode the bits, so they're not always used. If you need bit-level control, it's just as well to use bit operations to manipulate flags in a byte, although it may be a little less readable.

The formation will only be marching in one direction at a time: either left, right, or shifting down a row. The `MarchMode` struct handles these cases:

```
typedef struct {
  byte right:1; // 0 = left, 1 = right
  byte down:1;  // 0 = left/right, 1 = down
} MarchMode;

MarchMode this_mode, next_mode;
```

13.2 The Game Loop

> *p->name*
>
> Indexes the field *name* of the struct at pointer *p*.

To do things with `Enemy` structs, we often pass pointers to them. We can access the struct's fields with the `->` operator. It works just like the `.` operator but for pointers. For example, to draw an enemy, we might call this function:

```
void draw_enemy(Enemy* e) {
  draw_sprite(e->shape, e->x, e->y);
}
```

13. Game: Cosmic Impalas

Without ->, we'd have to use the * dereference operator:

```
draw_sprite((*e).shape, (*e).x, (*e).y); // yuck
```

When we start a level, we draw the playfield:

```
void draw_playfield() {
  byte i;
  // clear the screen to black
  clrscr();
  // draw score and # of lives
  draw_string("PLAYER 1", 0, 31);
  draw_score(0);
  draw_lives(0);
  // draw three horizontal lines at the bottom
  for (i=0; i<224; i++)
    vidmem[i][0] = 0x55;
  // draw bunkers at left and right of screen
  draw_bunker(30, 40, 15, 15, 20);
  draw_bunker(140, 40, 15, 15, 20);
}
```

Our main loop looks like this:

```
player_x = 96;          // set player horiz. position
bullet_y = 0;           // turn off player bullet
bomb_y = 0;             // turn off enemy bomb
frame = 0;              // zero frame counter
// loop until player is destroyed,
// or until we run out of enemies
while (player_x != 0xff && num_enemies) {
  move_player();        // move the player ship, fire
  if (bullet_y) {
    move_bullet();      // move the plyr bullet, chk collision
  }
  update_next_enemy();  // move a single enemy in formation
  if (frame & 1) { // run every odd frame
    if (bomb_y == 0) {
      drop_bomb();      // enemy drops bomb
    } else {
      move_bomb();      // enemy bomb moves, check collision
    }
  }
  watchdog_strobe = 0; // pet the watchdog
  frame++;
}
```

13.2. The Game Loop

`update_next_enemy` moves a single enemy at a time, so that updating the full formation of 28 enemies takes about a second. As enemies are destroyed, the enemy list shrinks, which makes the enemy formation move even faster!

```c
void update_next_enemy() {
  Enemy* e;
  // if we have moved the last enemy, start from the beginning
  if (enemy_index >= num_enemies) {
    enemy_index = 0;
    // can't assign struct to struct in SDCC (bummer!)
    memcpy(&this_mode, &next_mode, sizeof(this_mode));
  }
  // erase the current enemy
  e = &enemies[enemy_index];
  clear_sprite(e->shape, e->x, e->y);
  // enemy moving downward?
  if (this_mode.down) {
    // if too close to ground, end game
    if (--e->y < 5) {
      destroy_player();
      lives = 0;
    }
    next_mode.down = 0; // stop moving downward
  } else {
    // enemy moving right?
    if (this_mode.right) {
      e->x += 2;
      if (e->x >= 200) {
        next_mode.down = 1;  // move downward
        next_mode.right = 0; // afterwards, march right
      }
    } else {
      // enemy is moving left
      e->x -= 2;
      if (e->x == 0) {
        next_mode.down = 1;  // move downward
        next_mode.right = 1; // afterwards, march right
      }
    }
  }
  // now that it has moved, draw it again
  draw_sprite(e->shape, e->x, e->y);
  enemy_index++; // advance to next enemy
}
```

13. Game: Cosmic Impalas

In `move_player`, we read player inputs and decide whether to move the player left and right and/or fire a bullet. We also call `draw_sprite` to draw the player's new position, whether or not they moved (the sprite for the player has 2 lines of blanks on either side, so we don't have to erase as long as we don't move more than 2 pixels to either side):

```
void move_player() {
  if (attract) {
    // attract mode only
    if (bullet_y == 0) fire_bullet();
  } else {
    // read player left/right inputs
    if (LEFT1 && player_x>0) player_x -= 2;
    if (RIGHT1 && player_x<198) player_x += 2;
    // fire bullet if button pressed and no bullet onscreen
    if (FIRE1 && bullet_y == 0) {
      fire_bullet();
    }
  }
  draw_sprite(player_bitmap, player_x, 1); // draw player
}
```

13.3 Collision Detection

In our game, we want to see if missiles from the player hit the enemies, and if bombs from the enemies hit the player. There are generally three ways to go about this:

1. Use the video hardware's collision detector circuit (the Atari VCS has this, as well as some later platforms)

2. Compute the collisions in code, using bounding box intersection tests or some other method.

3. Test the frame buffer directly to see if the pixels of two shapes overlap.

For this game, we're going to use methods #3 and #2. When drawing a projectile, we'll see if it overlaps any existing pixels — this indicates that it's about to hit a player, enemy, or other obstacle. Then we see if the bullet's location intersects

13.3. Collision Detection

the bounding box (enclosing rectangle) of the player or any enemies, and if so, we destroy them in the appropriate manner.

We can tweak our xor_sprite method to detect leftover pixels. Remember that a shape drawn twice with XOR will reverse the first XOR'ed shape. If any pixels are left over after the second XOR, we must have overlapped something.

After we perform the exclusive-or and write back to the screen, we combine that with a result variable:

```
result |= (*dest++ ^= *src++);
```

That's a strange expression, isn't it? An assignment operator can be used as part of another expression, so the above is equivalent to:

```
*dest ^= *src++;
result |= *dest;
dest++;
```

If result is non-zero, we know that there were pixels left over after XOR-erasing the shape, and that our shape collided with something.

Now, we just have to figure out what we collided with! In our game, we put collision detection code in two places. The first is the routine that checks to see if the player's bullet hit something:

```
void move_bullet() {
  byte leftover = xor_sprite(bullet_bitmap, bullet_x,
    bullet_y); // erase
  // did we hit something, or did the bullet exit the top of
    the screen?
  if (leftover || bullet_y > 26) {
    clear_sprite(bullet_bitmap, bullet_x, bullet_y);
    check_bullet_hit(bullet_x, bullet_y+2); // look for hit
    bullet_y = 0; // get rid of bullet
  } else {
    // move bullet upwards
    bullet_y++;
    xor_sprite(bullet_bitmap, bullet_x, bullet_y); // draw
  }
}
```

13. Game: Cosmic Impalas

Note the use of xor_sprite — we XOR the sprite once to erase the old position, then again to draw the new position. If there were any leftover pixels after erasing the sprite, we check to see if there was a collision, calling check_bullet_hit to iterate through the enemy list.

When an enemy is hit, we have to delete it from the enemies array with delete_enemy:

```
void delete_enemy(Enemy* e) {
  // erase enemy
  clear_sprite(e->shape, e->x, e->y);
  // move list up one slit
  memmove(e, e+1, sizeof(Enemy)*(MAX_ENEMIES-1-(e-enemies)));
  num_enemies--;
}
```

The above memmove expression is a mouthful. Our goal is to slide up all of the array entries following the entry to be deleted. This diagram hopefully makes it more clear:

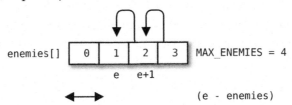

Figure 13.2: Deleting an entry in an array

The expression (e - enemies) is another case of *pointer arithmetic*. It's a way to convert the pointer e back into an array index. Also, we use the memmove function instead of memcpy because our source and destination ranges overlap.

The second place that checks collisions is move_bomb, which detects whether the enemy bomb hit something:

```
void move_bomb() {
  // erase bomb at old position
  byte leftover = xor_sprite(bomb_bitmap, bomb_x, bomb_y);
  if (bomb_y < 2) { // bomb hit the ground?
    bomb_y = 0;
  } else if (leftover) { // pixels leftover
    erase_sprite(bomb_bitmap, bomb_x, bomb_y); // erase bunker
    if (bomb_y == 2) {
      destroy_player();   // player was hit
    }
    bomb_y = 0; // get rid of bomb
  } else {
    bomb_y--; // move bomb down and redraw
    xor_sprite(bomb_bitmap, bomb_x, bomb_y);
  }
}
```

This routine is a lot like move_bullet, but goes in the other direction.

The bomb only hits the player's ship if a collision is detected when the bomb's Y position is exactly 2. Any higher up, and it's a bunker. Any lower, and it's the ground. (This is a very "iffy" test, but it works. If the bomb sprite were more than 8 pixels high, it might not — it's left to the reader to figure out why!)

13.4 Animating an Explosion

The routine that animates the player's explosion (or "de-rez" as we'll call it) is kinda neat. We want to pretend the player's ship teleported out of existence, and we use XOR heavily:

```
void destroy_player() {
  // animate the derez pattern with XOR (1st time)
  xor_player_derez();
  // XOR the player's ship, which erases it
  xor_sprite(player_bitmap, player_x, 1);
  // erase the derez pattern with XOR (2nd time)
  xor_player_derez();
  // get rid of player, decrement lives
  player_x = 0xff;
  lives--;
}
```

13. Game: Cosmic Impalas

The `xor_player_derez` function writes random dots with XOR inside the player's rectangle, starting at the bottom of the sprite and working its way up to 32 pixels of height. As a source of randomness, we define an array starting at address $0 – which happens to be the bytes of code in the ROM, random enough for our purposes!

```
void xor_player_derez() {
  byte i,j;
  byte x = player_x+13;
  byte y = 8;
  byte* rand = 0; // start of ROM
  for (j=1; j<=0x1f; j++) {
    for (i=0; i<50; i++) {
      // get next 'random' values for x/y coordinates
      char xx = x + (*rand++ & 0x1f) - 15;
      char yy = y + (*rand++ & j); // mask y with j
      xor_pixel(xx, yy); // draw pixel
    }
  }
}
```

The `xor_pixel` routine is pretty simple too. We make it `inline`, which saves a few bytes of code:

```
inline void xor_pixel(byte x, byte y) {
  // find the byte inside the scanline (y / 8)
  byte* dest = &vidmem[x][y>>3];
  // shift bit by (y % 8)
  *dest ^= 1 << (y & 7);
}
```

14

Interrupts

14.1 Interrupts

The Z80 can receive *interrupts*, which are external signals that tell the CPU to stop what it's doing and execute a specific code routine.

Each platform has its own way of generating and handling interrupts. In the Midway 8080 platform, there are two distinct interrupts: one when the video generator reaches scanline 96 (1/3 of the way across the frame) and one at scanline 224 (the end of the frame).

The Z80 has three different ways of responding to an interrupt signal; this platform uses *Mode 0 interrupts*. They work like this: When the Z80 receives an interrupt signal, it reads a single instruction off of the data bus — placed there by the signaling device — and then executes that instruction.

The instruction can only consist of a single byte. So what good can it be? As it turns out, the Z80 has a handy instruction called RST which jumps to a specific location in low memory. There are eight different versions of RST, which jump to address $00, $08, $10 and so on up to $38.

The Midway 8080 platform generates RST $08 and RST $10 instructions, so we have to make sure we have two interrupt routines, one starting at address $08 and one starting at $10.

The tricky thing about our C compiler is that it, unlike the assembler, does not allow us to set specific addresses for our

14. INTERRUPTS

routines. But with some care, we can write our routines so they line up at the proper locations.

In C, we first declare our two interrupt handlers with a special keyword, and our main function:

```
void scanline96() __interrupt;
void scanline224() __interrupt;
void main();
```

Now we have to carefully write our functions so that they conform to this memory map:

```
$0000    Start routine
$0008    Interrupt entry point for scanline 96
$0010    Interrupt entry point for scanline 224
```

First, we write the start routine, using some *inline assembly* (as described in Chapter 6) to set up the stack pointer and enable interrupts with the EI instruction:

```
void start() {
__asm
        LD      SP,#0x2400
        EI
        NOP
__endasm;
        main();
}
```

This translates into the following assembly output:

```
0000 31 00 24    [10]  116    LD      SP,#0x2400
0003 FB          [ 4]  117    EI
0004 00          [ 4]  118    NOP
0005 C3 D1 0B    [10]  120    jp      _main
```

Note that the routine ends at address $0007, meaning the next routine starts at address $0008. We've only got 8 bytes until the RST $10 handler starts, so we have to put a quick "trampoline" to the scanline96 handler which will be defined later:

14.1. Interrupts

```
void _RST_8() {
__asm
        NOP
        NOP
        NOP
        NOP
        NOP
__endasm;
        scanline96();
}
```

This translates into the following output:

```
   0008                              125 __RST_8::
   0008 00              [ 4]  127        NOP
   0009 00              [ 4]  128        NOP
   000A 00              [ 4]  129        NOP
   000B 00              [ 4]  130        NOP
   000C 00              [ 4]  131        NOP
   000D C3 1F 00        [10]  133        jp    _scanline96
```

This routine does nothing except jump to the scanline96 function — we don't have enough space to do much else, since we only have 8 bytes of room.

Because the previous routine ends at address $000F$, we can now define the RST $10 handler:

```
void scanline224() __interrupt {
}
```

Here, we just define the scanline224 function, which was defined with the __interrupt keyword. This causes the compiler to generate special entry and exit code, which looks like this:

```
   0010                              138 _scanline224::
   0010 FB              [ 4]  139        ei
   0011 F5              [11]  140        push    af
   0012 C5              [11]  141        push    bc
   0013 D5              [11]  142        push    de
   0014 E5              [11]  143        push    hl
   0015 FD E5           [15]  144        push    iy
                               145 ; ... your code goes here ...
   0017 FD E1           [14]  146        pop     iy
```

14. INTERRUPTS

```
0019 E1           [10]  147    pop    hl
001A D1           [10]  148    pop    de
001B C1           [10]  149    pop    bc
001C F1           [10]  150    pop    af
001D ED 4D        [14]  151    reti
```

This is boilerplate interrupt handler code. It pushes all of the register pairs (5 16-bit registers, or 10 8-bit registers in all) to the stack before the function starts, and pops them back from the stack before the function exits. Because the interrupt can happen while executing any bit of code, we must preserve all the registers so that the code that was interrupted doesn't get confused.

It also uses a RETI instruction at the end instead of RET. (The EI instruction at the beginning is for systems with stackable interupts, which doesn't apply to us.)

We can now define the scanline96 function, which will be used by the RST $08 handler defined earlier:

```
void scanline96() __interrupt {
}
```

It will have the same PUSH and POP boilerplate code as the other interrupt function.

Right now, these interrupt handlers don't do anything. We'll use interrupts in Chapter 18 to synchronize our screen writes with the raster beam so that we avoid flicker.

> Many programs, including the original *Space Invaders*, use the interrupt handlers to execute jobs from a task list. This design ensures that animated objects are drawn every frame and also out of the way of the raster beam. In the examples in this book, we use the interrupt routines only for counting frames and draw everything in the main loop.

15

Randomness

Most games have a need to generate random numbers. Maybe the game needs an enemy that behaves unpredictably, or requires that a game element appears at random positions on the screen. This is usually accomplished by using a *pseudorandom number generator* (PRNG). This is an algorithm that starts from a number called a *seed* and modifies it in a complex way to generate successive random numbers.

If designed correctly, the PRNG will cycle through a large range of values that do not repeat themselves, or only repeat after many thousands of iterations. This is called the *period* of the PRNG.

A common type of PRNG is a *linear-feedback shift register (LFSR)* which combines shifts with bit operations to generate numbers. The operations are usually carefully chosen to maximize the period of the sequence. For math reasons, only 16 different 8-bit LFSRs have the maximal period of 255 values (zero is not allowed, otherwise it'd be 256). This means it'll cycle through every non-zero 8-bit number exactly once, in a seemingly haphazard order, until it repeats.

LFSRs were popular in early computer and video game designs, since they are easily implemented in hardware. They operate as simple counters, produce audio noise, even generate video (the Galaxian starfield comes from a 17-bit LFSR.) They're also easy to implement in software, as we'll see.

15. Randomness

15.1 Galois LFSR

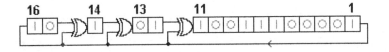

Figure 15.1: 16-bit Galois LFSR

A *Galois LFSR* is a perhaps the most simply-implemented variety of LFSR. The routine below produces $2^{16} - 1$ (65535) values – all 16-bit values except zero.

```
word lfsr = 1;

word rand() {
  byte lsb = lfsr & 1;
  lfsr >>= 1;
  if (lsb) lfsr ^= 0xd400;
  return lfsr;
}
```

Since half of the time a Galois LFSR just performs a simple shift, you may have to iterate at least twice to get plausible-looking random values. Because the period of a maximal LFSR is odd, you can iterate twice and still get the full range of values.

Many LFSRs are also reversible, i.e., the sequence can be run backwards. The reverse of the LFSR shown above uses the constant $a801 (the previous constant rotated left by 1 bit):

```
word rev_rand() {
  byte lsb = (lfsr & 0x8000) != 0;
  lfsr <<= 1;
  if (lsb) lfsr ^= 0xa801;
  return lfsr;
}
```

Another cheap source of pseudo-randomness is to just read bytes from the code in the ROM directly. The random-ish nature of the machine instructions will be good enough for some applications, like a noisy video or audio signal. We used this technique in Chapter 13 to draw a random field of dots.

15.2 Entropy

If you find your random numbers are too predictable, you could add *entropy* to your PRNG. This is a source of uncertainty that makes your random number stream a little more unpredictable.

Some good sources for entropy:

- The player's control inputs
- A hardware clock or hardware PRNG
- A counter in a VSYNC wait loop

Here's a simple example of adding entropy by combining the LFSR value with a controller input. Since our Galois generator doesn't like the value 0, we correct it to 1 when we find it:

```
function add_entropy() {
  lfsr ^= input1;
  if (!lfsr) lfsr = 1;
}
```

While this might make your RNG more unpredictable, it won't neccessarily make it non-repeatable! If the addition of entropy makes the LFSR return to a previous value, it'll emit the same sequence again. But we're playing games, not generating cryptographic keys. Experimentation will likely tell you what works and what doesn't.

16

Initializing Memory

16.1 Initialized vs. Uninitialized vs. Const

Consider the following variables:

```
int uninit_value;
const int const_value = 0x123;
int init_value = 0x7f;
```

All three lines declare integers, but each is treated differently by the compiler, and will be put in different *segments* (our assembler calls them *areas*, but *segment* is more common).

The first is an *uninitialized* declaration:

```
int uninit_value;
```

This gets placed into our _DATA segment, where uninitalized values live in RAM. These don't get set to any particular value on startup – in our emulator, they'll be set initially to zeroes.

The assembler defines our variable like this:

```
                         28           .area _DATA
      2000               29 _uninit_value::
      2000               30           .ds 2
```

This allocates two bytes in the _DATA segment for `uninit_value`.

The next declaration is a *const* value:

```
const int const_value = 0x123;
```

16. Initializing Memory

The const keyword indicates that value can't be changed — it's *constant*. The compiler will place it in the _CODE segment and assign it a value:

```
                          57           .area _CODE
0000                      58  _const_value:
0000 41 01                59           .dw #0x0123
```

The last line is an *initialized* declaration, which is assigned a value on startup and from that point can be changed:

`int init_value = 0x7f;`

This variable will be placed into the _INITIALIZED segment. It lives in RAM just like the _DATA segment, but it is initialized on startup as we'll see below. First, two bytes are allocated in the _INITIALIZED segment:

```
                          34           .area _INITIALIZED
2002                      35  _init_value::
2002                      36           .ds 2
```

The actual value (0x007f) is placed into the _INITIALIZER segment:

```
                          60           .area _INITIALIZER
0002                      61  __xinit__init_value:
0002 7B 00                62           .dw #0x007f
```

106

16.2 Initializing Memory

In our bare-bones compiler pipeline, we omit the entry routine that in other C systems performs housekeeping duties like initializing memory. So we'll have to do it ourselves:

```
// start routine @ 0x0
void start() {
__asm
; set up stack pointer, interrupt flag
        LD    SP,#0xE800
        DI
; copy initialized data
        LD    BC, #l__INITIALIZER
        LD    A, B
        LD    DE, #s__INITIALIZED
        LD    HL, #s__INITIALIZER
        LDIR
__endasm;
        main();
}
```

The inline assembly code under the "copy initialized data" comment just copies the entire contents of _INITIALIZER segment into the _INITIALIZED segment. The identifiers with the l_ and s_ prefixes are added by the assembler, and they represent the length and origin of the given segment.

The compiler sets up both segments so that this operation effectively initializes all of the values in the _INITIALIZED segment.

16. Initializing Memory

16.3 Initializing Strings vs. Arrays

Strings and arrays are similar, but not identical. Consider these two declarations:

```
const char* const DIGITS = "0123456789";

const char DIGITARRAY[10] = {
    '0','1','2','3','4','5','6','7','8','9' };
```

At first glance, the string DIGITS and the array DIGITARRAY produce the same bytes. But the string has an extra zero byte at the end, because it is null-terminated.

Also, the string DIGITS is an actual pointer — there is a 16-bit value in the ROM pointing to the first digit. DIGITARRAY is an aggregate type, so although it is coerced to a pointer when used in an expression, its size is 10 bytes, not 2.

One odd thing in the declaration for DIGITS: why did we say const twice? Since DIGITS declares two objects — a string of bytes, and a pointer to those bytes — we need to declare the pointer itself to be constant, too. If we removed the second const, we could say:

```
DIGITS = NULL;
```

This would work, too. Since the pointer is not declared const, the compiler would put the DIGITS pointer into the initialized RAM segment, not in ROM. This would also be very confusing if we happened to forget to initialize RAM in the start function!

17

The Galaxian Hardware

17.1 History

Namco's first game was *Gee Bee*, a pinball-inspired breakout-style game. *Galaxian* was their follow-up, inspired by the recently released *Space Invaders* as well as the first *Star Wars* movie.[8]

The *Galaxian* hardware pushed the limit of video game designs in 1979. At its core is a Z80 CPU at 3.072 MHz. The graphics system featured color RGB graphics and multicolor hardware sprites overlapping a tiled background. (At the time, the term "sprite" had not yet been coined, so designers called them "stamps.")

The designers would reuse the same PCB (printed circuit board) for *King & Balloon*, and also for the legendary sequel *Galaga*. Other companies like Konami licensed the video hardware to make games like *Scramble* and *Frogger*.

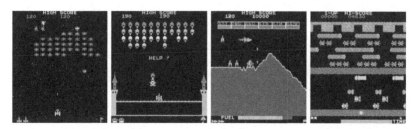

Figure 17.1: Galaxian, King & Balloon, Scramble, and Frogger

17. The Galaxian Hardware

The *Scramble* hardware was a popular target for ports and bootlegs of other Z80-based games. *Crazy Kong* for instance was a bootleg of *Donkey Kong*, identical except for the color palette and sound. Even *Scramble* itself was hacked to run on older *Galaxian* hardware!

Galaxian uses a 32x28 tilemap like the VIC Dual hardware, but each column can be assigned separate color attributes. Also, individual columns can be scrolled left and right, or up and down if the monitor is in landscape orientation.

Galaxian's sprites are 16x16 bitmaps with three colors (plus one transparent color) that can be positioned anywhere on the screen. They overlap the background tilemap and also each other. Galaxian uses sprites for attacking aliens — for aliens in formation, tiles are used, along with the column-scrolling feature to move them around. There can be up to eight sprites on a given scanline.

There are also eight "bullets" that can be separately positioned and show up on the screen as short vertical lines (on *Scramble* hardware, they show up as single pixels). Only two bullets can appear on a given scanline. Bullet #7 — the player's bullet — appears as a separate color and has priority over the others.

 To see it on 8bitworkshop.com: Select the **Scramble Hardware** platform, then select the **Graphics Test** file.

17.2 Memory Map

We've chosen the *Scramble* memory map for our emulator — it's similar to Galaxian and used as the basis for many other games:

Start	End	Description	R/W
$0000	$3FFF	ROM	read
$4000	$47FF	program RAM	r/w
$4800	$4BFF	video RAM	write
$4C00	$4FFF	video RAM (mirror)	write
$5000	$50FF	object RAM	write
$6801		enable interrupt	write
$6803		enable blue background	write
$6804		enable stars	write
$7000		watchdog timer	read
$8100		input 0	read
$8101		input 1	read
$8102		input 2	read

Table 17.1: Scramble Memory Map

The Galaxian hardware is similar except for these changes:

Start	End	Description	R/W
$6000		input 0	read
$6800		input 1	read
$7000		input 2	read
$7800		watchdog timer	read
$7001		enable interrupt	write
$7004		enable stars	write

Table 17.2: Galaxian Memory Map

The tilemap is defined as a 32x32 byte array, defined here as the variable vram:

```
byte __at (0x4800) vram[32][32]; // 32x32 cells
```

Each byte selects one of the 256 available tiles.

17. The Galaxian Hardware

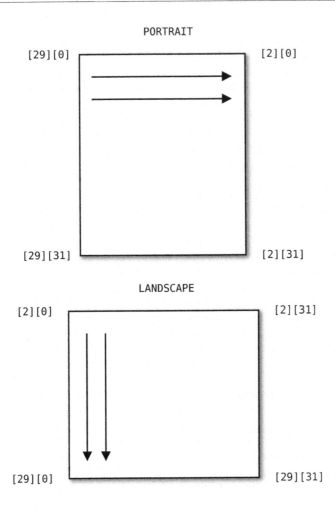

Figure 17.2: Galaxian video RAM layout

Some of the tiles are offscreen. In portrait orientation, the leftmost two and rightmost two columns are hidden. If you want to hide sprites or missiles, you can position them in this area.

The other section of video RAM, "object RAM," has a more complex structure. We'll use arrays of C structs to define each section.

17.2. Memory Map

First we'll define the column registers. There are 32 columns, each having a scroll and attrib byte (for a total of 64 bytes):

```
struct {
  byte scroll;  // column scroll position
  byte attrib;  // column attribute (color set)
} __at (0x5000) vcolumns[32];
```

(In portrait orientation, the columns are rotated 90 degrees, so they are actually horizontal rows. But we call them columns anyway.)

The scroll byte moves an entire column of tiles to the right by the given number of pixels, wrapping the remainder to the other side. Refer to Figure 17.2 and note that four tiles (32 pixels) will always be partially or completely hidden.

The attrib byte controls the colors used by the column. The palette is set up as 8 sets with 4 colors in each set, so this byte picks out one of the 8 sets. Like the VIC Dual system, it's contained in a *PROM*, which we've mapped to $5000 in the emulator ROM:

```
// palette entry macro (red 0-7, green 0-7, blue 0-3)
#define PE(r,g,b) ((r)|((g)<<3)|((b)<<6))

const char __at (0x5000) palette[32] = {
  0,PE(0,0,0),PE(0,0,0),PE(6,6,3),
  0,PE(7,1,1),PE(0,0,3),PE(7,7,3),
  ...
};
```

Each of the 16 palette entries contains a single byte, mapped to RGB values like so:

```
Bit   76543210
Color BBGGGRRR
```

17. The Galaxian Hardware

The 8 hardware sprites each use 4 bytes of object RAM:

```
struct {
  byte xpos;     // x position
  byte code;     // tile index
  byte color;    // color set index
  byte ypos;     // y position
} __at (0x5040) vsprites[8];
```

The xpos and ypos bytes define the X and Y coordinate of the sprite. We've defined these here as valid for portrait orientation — X goes from left to right, and Y goes from top to bottom. The same visibility rules apply as for tiles, so X = 0 and X = 240 are both offscreen.

The code byte selects which tiles to use for the sprite. Sprites are 16x16, so they use four 8x8 tiles, which are chosen by adding code to the offsets in Figure 17.3.

The color byte selects the color palette of the sprite from the 8 different color sets, similar to how it's done for tiles.

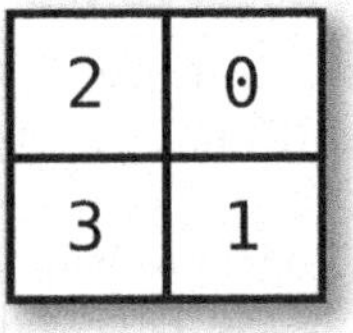

The missiles or bullets are defined similarly to sprites, except they only have X and Y coordinates:

2	0
3	1

Figure 17.3: Galaxian sprite layout

```
struct {
  byte unused1;
  byte xpos;     // x position
  byte unused2;
  byte ypos;     // y position (inverted)
} __at (0x5060) vmissiles[8];
```

The Y coordinate is inverted, and an offset is applied which depends on the exact hardware. On *Scramble* hardware, Y = 249 is the top of the screen, and Y = 0 is six pixels from the bottom. So to hide missiles, you should set Y to 255, or X to 0.

17.3 Other Special Addresses

The `enable_irq` switch can be set to 1 to activate interrupts. This causes the video hardware to generate a non-maskable interrupt (NMI) once per frame. The interrupt handler must live at address $66 in the ROM. We'll show you how to write interrupt handlers in Chapter 18.

```
byte __at (0x6801) enable_irq;
```

The `enable_starts` switch is fun. When set to 1, it shows blinking stars! These are generated by a hardware circuit on the actual PCB.

```
byte __at (0x6804) enable_stars;
```

This system also has a watchdog timer that must be read (not written to) at least once every 8 video frames (8/60 = 0.133 seconds). Here's one easy way to do this in C:

```
watchdog++;
```

This performs a read of the watchdog, resetting it, and then a write which is ignored.

Finally, there are three input latches for joysticks, buttons, coin counters, and DIP switches.

```
byte __at (0x8100) input0;
byte __at (0x8101) input1;
byte __at (0x8102) input2;

#define LEFT1  !(input0 & 0x20)
#define RIGHT1 !(input0 & 0x10)
#define UP1    !(input0 & 0x1)
#define DOWN1  !(input2 & 0x40)
#define FIRE1  !(input0 & 0x8)
#define BOMB1  !(input0 & 0x2)
#define COIN1  !(input0 & 0x80)
#define COIN2  !(input0 & 0x40)
#define START1 !(input1 & 0x80)
#define START2 !(input1 & 0x40)
```

17.4 Graphics ROMs

In the actual arcade game, the tile graphic data is in separate ROMs. In the emulator, they're tacked onto the end of the program ROM — so we expect them at a certain offset, $4000. This is easy to do with the __at keyword in SDCC:

```
const char __at (0x4000) tilerom[0x1000] = {
...
};
```

The 256 tiles in the ROM are arranged just like those in the VIC Dual system, but there are two separate *bitplanes*. The bits in each plane are combined to produce a 4-bit color for each tile pixel.

The color palette is in a programmable ROM chip (PROM). The emulator expects the data at address $5000:

```
const char __at (0x5000) color_prom[32] = {
... 32 bytes ...
};
```

17.5 Sound

Galaxian has a separate sound PCB with discrete circuits based on 555 timers and other counters. Later games like *Scramble* often had a dedicated sound CPU, usually another Z80. The main CPU would communicate with the sound CPU via a programmable peripheral interface chip like the Intel 8255.

To make things simpler, we're going to pretend that there are two AY-3-8910 PSGs hooked up directly to the main CPU via I/O ports. They are connected similarly to the VIC Dual sound ports:

```
__sfr __at (0x1) ay8910_a_reg;
__sfr __at (0x2) ay8910_a_data;
__sfr __at (0x4) ay8910_b_reg;
__sfr __at (0x8) ay8910_b_data;
```

17.6. When Not to Use memset()

```
inline void set8910a(byte reg, byte data) {
  ay8910_a_reg = reg;
  ay8910_a_data = data;
}

inline void set8910b(byte reg, byte data) {
  ay8910_b_reg = reg;
  ay8910_b_data = data;
}
```

17.6 When Not to Use memset()

We might want to clear the screen by filling the entire frame buffer with a blank character tile. So we might try to use memset like this:

```
memset(vram, 0x10, sizeof(vram));
```

If we tried this, we'd see garbage instead of a clear screen. What gives?

The Z80 has a special instruction, LDIR, that can copy a range of bytes to another location. The C compiler uses this instruction for memcpy and memmove. The memset routine uses it too, but it sets a single zero in memory, then LDIR copies that zero to all subsequent locations.

Here's the problem: on this platform we can't read from video memory (vram, sprites, etc), only write. So when LDIR tries to copy our target byte, it'll read zeroes, or garbage bytes.

Instead, we use our own memset_safe routine for video and object RAM, which only writes to these regions:

```
void memset_safe(void* _dest, char ch, word size) {
  byte* dest = _dest;
  while (size--) {
    *dest++ = ch;
  }
}
```

18

Game: Solarian

We're going to make another game! We'll call it *Solarian* (since our enemies are local to the solar system, not from another galaxy or anything...)

> To see it on 8bitworkshop.com: Select the **Scramble Hardware** platform, then select the **Solarian Game** file.

In Solarian, enemies will be in one of two primary states: in formation, or flying around. For enemies in formation, their position will be implied by its position in the array, as seen in Figure 18.1.

Figure 18.1: Array indices of enemies in formation

18. Game: Solarian

So we really only need a single byte for each `FormationEnemy`, to tell us if it is present and what shape to draw:

```
typedef struct {
  byte shape;  // shape code
} FormationEnemy;
```

The attacking enemies have more complex state. They have arbitrary X and Y coordinates, and can fly in multiple directions. We also want to track their original formation index so they can return to their original positions. The `AttackingEnemy` struct looks like this:

```
// should be power of 2 length
typedef struct {
  byte findex;    // formation index
  byte shape;     // shape code
  word x;         // X position (* 256)
  word y;         // Y position (* 256)
  byte dir;       // direction (0-31)
  byte returning; // 1 = back to formation
} AttackingEnemy;

AttackingEnemy attackers[MAX_ATTACKERS];
```

You might ask why the X and Y coordinates are 16-bit (`word` type) instead of 8-bit, when our screen coordinates only go as high as 255. These will be treated as 16-bit *fixed-point* values. This means that we treat some of the bits in the value as fractional. In this case, we consider the entire lower byte to be 1/256th of its integer value. It's like putting an invisible decimal point between each 8 bits of the 16-bit value, between the two bytes:

```
Hi Byte   Lo Byte
----------------
NNNNNNNN.ffffffff
```

To turn an integer into a fixed-point value, we simply shift left by 8 bits, which is the same as multiplying by 256:

```
xx = x << 8;
```

Similarly, we can extract the integer part of the fixed-point value by shifting right by 8 bits:

```
x = xx >> 8;
```

Our C compiler is smart enough to know that when you shift a 16-bit value by 8 bits, all you have to do is load the high byte of the value. So shifting by 8 bits doesn't take any extra time at all.

If we want the fractional value, we just extract the lower byte, maybe with a bitmask:

```
xfrac = fpx & 0xff;    // use bitmask
xfrac = (byte)fpx;     // same thing
```

18.1 Drawing Tiles vs. Sprites

The Galaxian hardware only supports 8 sprites at a time, but we want to have dozens of enemies on the screen. The hardware has a clever solution for this: just use the background tiles for enemies in formation, and only use sprites when enemies are flying around.

Since the hardware has column scroll support (this translates to scrolling horizontal rows when the screen is rotated), we can move entire rows of enemies left to right.

18. Game: Solarian

We can make it seamless enough that the player won't notice when an enemy takes flight and transitions from background tile to sprite, and potentially back again.

```
void draw_row(byte row) {
  byte i;
  byte y = 4 + row * 2; // compute row position
  // set palette entry for row
  columns[y].attrib = 0x2;
  // set scroll position for row (global variable)
  columns[y].scroll = formation_offset_x;
  // loop over all enemies
  for (i=0; i<ENEMIES_PER_ROW; i++) {
    byte x = i * 3; // tile position within row
    byte shape = formation[i + row*ENEMIES_PER_ROW].shape;
    // is an enemy present in this space?
    if (shape) {
      putchar(x, y, shape);     // left side
      putchar(x+1, y, shape-2); // right side
    } else {
      putchar(x, y, BLANK);     // left side
      putchar(x+1, y, BLANK);   // right side
    }
  }
}
```

To save CPU cycles, we draw the formation rows individually, only drawing one row per frame. The formation will slowly shimmy from side-to-side, but fast enough that the player won't see individual rows being moved.

Even the player can be drawn with tiles — 2x2 tiles give us a 16x16 pixel shape:

```
columns[29].attrib = 1;
columns[30].attrib = 1;
vram[30][29] = 0x60;
vram[31][29] = 0x62;
vram[30][30] = 0x61;
vram[31][30] = 0x63;
```

Figure 18.2: Visualization of ship drawn in tile columns 29 and 30

There is nothing else on the rows that contain the player's ship, so to move it back and forth we just set the column positions like so:

```
columns[29].scroll = player_x;
columns[30].scroll = player_x;
```

This gives us a lot of flexibility without requiring us to add additional sprites. For instance, we could draw a second ship next to the first, or we could create a big 4x4 explosion using tiles.

18.2 Attack!

When we want a alien-in-formation to transition to an attacker (i.e., flying alien), we call the formation_to_attacker function, passing the formation index of the alien. Then we search through our attackers array for an empty slot, and fill in the details of our new attacker:

```
// find an empty attacker slot
for (i=0; i<MAX_ATTACKERS; i++) {
  AttackingEnemy* a = &attackers[i];
  if (a->findex == 0) {
    // set attacker details
    // translate x and y to fixed-point (* 256)
    a->x = get_attacker_x(formation_index) << 8;
    a->y = get_attacker_y(formation_index) << 8;
    a->shape = formation[formation_index].shape;
    a->findex = formation_index+1;
    // clear the formation slot
    formation[formation_index].shape = 0;
    break;
  }
}
```

18. Game: Solarian

The `get_attacker_x` and `get_attacker_y` compute the X and Y coordinates of a sprite, given the formation index. It's just a matter of finding the row and column, then multiplying and adding some constants:

```
byte get_attacker_x(byte formation_index) {
  byte column = (formation_index % ENEMIES_PER_ROW);
  return FORMATION_XSPACE*column + FORMATION_X0 +
    formation_offset_x;
}

byte get_attacker_y(byte formation_index) {
  byte row = formation_index / ENEMIES_PER_ROW;
  return FORMATION_YSPACE*row + FORMATION_Y0);
}
```

---

x % y

Computes the *modulus* ($x \bmod y$) – basically the remainder of an integer division.

This is a slow operation on 8-bit platforms (like multiplication and division) unless y is a power-of-two and x is unsigned, in which case the compiler will usually replace it with a bitwise-and.

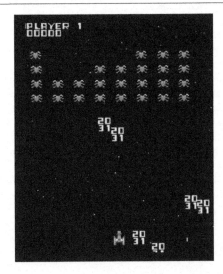

Figure 18.3: Enemy sprites, shown as numbers

18.3 Directions and Trig

We want aliens to be able to fly in any direction, so we need to track the angle that they are heading. We'll encode the angle as one of 32 different values — it's a power of two, which will be helpful.

To move an X,Y position D units along a vector with angle A, we generally do this:

```
X := X + sin(A) * D
Y := Y + cos(A) * D
```

Floating-point is very expensive in the 8-bit world, and we don't need nearly that much precision, so we'll cheat and use lookup tables.

Our lookup table has 32 values, one for each integer angle, and ranges from -127 to 127 (we generated this with a Python script):

```
const byte SINTBL[32] = {
  0, 25, 49, 71, 90, 106, 117, 125,
  127, 125, 117, 106, 90, 71, 49, 25,
  0, -25, -49, -71, -90, -106, -117, -125,
  -127, -125, -117, -106, -90, -71, -49, -25,
};
```

Our integer sin and cosine routines (`isin` and `icos`) become very simple:

```
signed char isin(byte dir) {
  return SINTBL[dir & 31];      // limit to 0-31
}

signed char icos(byte dir) {
  return isin(dir+8);           // offset 90 degrees
}
```

To move an alien a along its current heading `dir`, we just do this:

```
a->x += isin(a->dir) * 2;
a->y += icos(a->dir) * 2;
```

18. Game: Solarian

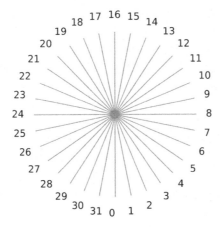

Figure 18.4: Compass directions of 32-byte sine table

Figure 18.5: Rotations of an enemy sprite

We multiply each value by 2, but you could use whatever value you want to make them move faster or slower. This value makes them move almost 1 pixel per frame.

We also we want different shapes to be displayed for each rotation angle. We don't have any rotation hardware, and limited ROM space for bitmaps.

Fortunately, we have hardware that can automatically flip sprites vertically and horizontally. This means we only need rotated versions of the sprite for 90 degrees of the rotation — since our scheme has 32 rotation values, that's no more than 8 distinct sprites.

We can easily use a lookup table to store the proper offset and flip flags for each of the 32 rotation values:

```
#define FLIPX 0x40
#define FLIPY 0x80
#define FLIPXY 0xc0
```

```
const byte DIR_TO_CODE[32] = {
  0, 1, 2, 3, 4, 5, 6, 6,
  6|FLIPXY, 6|FLIPXY, 5|FLIPXY, 4|FLIPXY, 3|FLIPXY, 2|FLIPXY,
    1|FLIPXY, 0|FLIPXY,
  0|FLIPX, 1|FLIPX, 2|FLIPX, 3|FLIPX, 4|FLIPX, 5|FLIPX,
    6|FLIPX, 6|FLIPX,
  6|FLIPY, 6|FLIPY, 5|FLIPY, 4|FLIPY, 3|FLIPY, 2|FLIPY,
    1|FLIPY, 0|FLIPY,
}; // note: we only have 7 rotated sprite bitmaps, not 8...
```

18.4 Alien Behavior

We'd like to give the aliens a sort of unpredictable behavior when they attack — zooming down the screen, then turning away to one side, dropping bombs as they go.

With a little experimentation, this can be easily done just by looking at the alien's position. When it is in the upper half of the screen, we rotate. When it arrives in the lower half, we start dropping bombs. We decide which way to rotate depending on whether it is in the left or right half of the screen.

```
// convert fixed-point to integer
byte x = a->x >> 8;
byte y = a->y >> 8;
// if in upper half of screen, rotate enemy
// but don't shoot missiles after player explodes
if (y < 128 || player_exploding) {
  // left half of screen?
  if (x < 112) {
    a->dir++; // turn clockwise
  } else {
    a->dir--; // counter-clockwise
  }
} else {
  // we're in lower half of screen
  // shoot a missile, if slot is available
  if (missiles[i].ypos == 0) {
    missiles[i].ypos = 245-y;
    missiles[i].xpos = x+8;
    missiles[i].dy = -2; // speed
  }
}
```

18.5 Returning To Formation

We'd like the aliens to smoothly swoop back into their previous position in the formation using the same direction-based algorithm, but that's pretty tricky. So we'll cheat, and use a different mode of travel when an alien is returning (We'll call the actual flag `returning`.)

In our `move_attackers` function, we'll choose one of two other functions based on this flag:

```
if (a->returning)
    return_attacker(a);      // return to formation
else
    fly_attacker(a);         // fly around
```

In `fly_attacker`, we see if the alien has wrapped around the bottom of the screen, and if so, we set the `returning` flag:

```
if ((a->y >> 8) == 0) {  // convert from fixed-point
    a->returning = 1;
}
```

In `return_attacker`, we slowly lower the alien into position, setting its X coordinate exactly where it needs to be, and slowly moving the Y coordinate downward. We also cleverly rotate the alien so it looks like it's flipping over into its space:

```
void return_attacker(AttackingEnemy* a) {
  byte fi = a->findex-1;
  byte destx = get_attacker_x(fi);
  byte desty = get_attacker_y(fi);
  byte ydist = desty - (a->y >> 8); // distance to slot
  // have we arrived at our formation slot?
  if (ydist == 0) {
    // convert back to formation enemy
    formation[fi].shape = a->shape;
    a->findex = 0; // disable attacker
  } else {
    // we're near our slot, set position and rotation
    a->dir = (ydist + 16) & 31;
    a->x = destx << 8;
    a->y += 128;
  }
}
```

When the alien reaches its target Y coordinate, we convert it back to a formation enemy — it'll no longer be a sprite, but it'll again be drawn as a pair of background tiles.

18.6 Missiles

Drawing missiles is simple, as they are supported as separate graphic entities in the hardware, like sprites. We can't read from the object RAM segment, so we're going to have to define our own "shadow" missile array:

```
typedef struct {
  signed char dx;      // delta-X change
  byte xpos;           // X coordinate
  signed char dy;      // delta-Y change
  byte ypos;           // Y coordinate
} Missile;

Missile missiles[8];
```

We'll use dy as the delta y-position (speed and direction) of the missile. Missiles have reversed Y coordinates from sprites, so position 0 is the bottom of the screen. We'll use 0 to mean a missile slot is "available" since it is also offscreen.

Here's the routine that moves missiles every frame:

```
void move_missiles() {
  byte i;
  for (i=0; i<8; i++) {
    if (missiles[i].ypos) {
      // move missile, and check to see if hit top of screen
      missiles[i].ypos += missiles[i].dy;
      if ((byte)missiles[i].ypos < 4) {
        missiles[i].xpos = 0xff; // hide offscreen
        missiles[i].ypos = 0;
      }
    }
  }
  // copy all "shadow missiles" to video memory
  memcpy(vmissiles, missiles, sizeof(missiles));
}
```

18. Game: Solarian

We use `memcpy` to copy our "shadow missiles" array to object RAM. We set up our `Missile` struct so that it's identical to the one in object RAM, except we're using the two unused bytes.

Since missiles move at varying speeds, we'll hide the missile when it comes within 4 pixels of the bottom (missiles that go upwards will wrap around to the bottom, and then be hidden).

> *(type) expression*
>
> Casts *expression* to the type *type*. This is a signal to the compiler to treat the expression as the given type. The compiler will produce an error if a type cast is not allowed.

Note the following expression:

```
((byte)missiles[i].ypos < 4)
```

But also note the `(byte)` at the beginning of the expression. This is called a *type cast*. In our missile struct, the `ypos` field is unsigned, but `dy` is signed. In C, this makes the result of the addition signed. Since signed bytes can only range from -128 to 127, we would overflow the signed byte halfway up the screen! We cast this expression to `byte` before doing the comparison so that we get the full 0-255 range, and take advantage of integer overflow. (We'll talk more about this in Chapter 20.)

18.7 Blowing Up Aliens

We reserve a dedicated sprite entry for exploding aliens, and when an alien explodes we activate it and move it wherever it needs to be:

```
void blowup_at(byte x, byte y) {
  vsprites[6].color = 1; // palette
  vsprites[6].code = 28; // explosion
  vsprites[6].xpos = x;
  vsprites[6].ypos = y;
  enemy_exploding = 1;
}

void animate_enemy_explosion() {
  if (enemy_exploding) {
    // animate next frame
```

```
    vsprites[6].code = 28 + enemy_exploding++;
    if (enemy_exploding > 4)
      enemy_exploding = 0; // hide explosion after 4 frames
  }
}
```

Then we animate the explosion every 4 frames:

```
if ((framecount & 3) == 0) animate_enemy_explosion();
```

18.8 Game Sound

Instead of scattering sound code all over the place, we're going to put it all in a single function. This will be called every 1/60 of a second in the main loop.

First we have an enable byte variable that tracks all of the sound channels activated so far. We'll use it later to set the ENABLE register:

```
void set_sounds() {
  byte enable = 0;
```

We want a sound when the player fires a missile, one that decreases in pitch and volume as the missile goes up the screen. We can use the sprite's ypos to set channel A's pitch and volume:

```
  if (missiles[7].ypos) {
    set8910a(AY_PITCH_A_LO, missiles[7].ypos);
    set8910a(AY_ENV_VOL_A, 15-(missiles[7].ypos>>4));
    enable |= 0x1; // channel A tone
  }
```

We also want a bleepy explosion sound when an enemy blows up — we'll vary the pitch based on the enemy_exploding variable:

```
  if (enemy_exploding) {
    set8910a(AY_PITCH_B_HI, enemy_exploding);
    set8910a(AY_ENV_VOL_B, 15);
    enable |= 0x2; // channel B tone
  }
```

We also want a big noisy boom in channel C when the player explodes, one that starts loud and quickly fades. We use the `player_exploding` variable for the volume. We have to set the 6th bit in the Enable register to mix the noise generator into Channel C:

```
if (player_exploding && player_exploding < 15) {
  set8910a(AY_ENV_VOL_C, 15-player_exploding);
  enable |= 0b00100000; // channel C noise
}
```

We've been keeping the Enable flags in a local variable. Next we actually set the Enable register, inverting all the bits since a 1 bit disables the corresponding channel, and a 0 bit enables it:

```
set8910a(AY_ENABLE, ~enable); // set enable flags
```

18.9 Keeping in Sync with Interrupts

We discussed Mode 0 interrupts in Chapter 13. This system uses another Z80 interrupt mode, Mode 2. In this mode, an interrupt always causes a jump to address $66.

Since our C compiler doesn't have a way to position functions, we have to add padding (unused bytes) until our interrupt routine is positioned exactly where we need — which is offset $66. We can do this using inline assembly at the end of the start function:

```
.ds   0x66 - (. - _start)
```

The `.ds` directive means "insert N bytes here." The expression (. - _start) is the assembler's program counter subtracted from the _start label. We do this to convert the program counter to an absolute constant (stuff specific to the SDCC assembler). Then we subtract that value from 0x66, which is the address where we want our interrupt handler to reside.

We also add the __naked function decorator so that the compiler doesn't insert a RET instruction or stack frame instructions, modifying our code length.

18.9. Keeping in Sync with Interrupts

Now that the compiler is positioned at the correct address, we can write the interrupt handler code. It'll run every time a VSYNC occurs at the start of each video frame, i.e., every 1/60 second. All it does right now is increment a counter variable:

```
volatile word video_framecount;

void rst_66() __interrupt {
  video_framecount++;    // increment video framecount
}
```

Since our main loop takes a variable number of CPU cycles depending on the activity on-screen, we need a way to keep our video frame rate consistent.

One solution is to keep another counter in our main loop. Then we simply compare the video counter against our game loop's framecount counter, and spin the CPU as long as they are equal:

```
void wait_for_frame() {
  while (((video_framecount^framecount) & 3) == 0);
}
```

As long as the game loop takes less than 1/60 second, the loop will stay in sync with the counter. But if our loop ever takes longer than that, the counter will go out of sync, and the main loop will no longer wait for the video sync signal. It'll get back in sync eventually.

We only compare the first two bits of the counters, so that it takes less time to get back in sync.

> On the Galaxian/Scramble platforms, the main loop must acknowledge an interrupt to allow interrupts to continue. This is done by setting `enable_irq` to 0 and then 1.

19

Making Music

Playing music on the AY-3-8910 is just a matter of setting the right frequencies at the right times (isn't that true of all music?)

> To see it on 8bitworkshop.com: Select the **VIC Dual** platform, then select the **Music Player** file.

19.1 Hitting the Right Note

First, we need to create a table that maps musical notes to their period register values. If we count the first key on a standard 88-key piano as 1, the frequency of a note is given by this equation:

$$F_{A4} \cdot \frac{2^{(note-49)}}{12}$$

F_{A4} is the frequency of the musical note A above middle C, often called A4 or A440, since its standard frequency is 440 Hz.

Since the Tone Period register can only store integer values, we cannot get all notes exactly on pitch. The tuning error increases rapidly as the notes get higher in pitch, since the integer divisor gets closer to zero.

However, we can choose a value for A4 to minimize the tuning error in a certain note range. Generally, we have to give up accuracy in higher frequencies to get more accurate lower frequencies. Compare the two charts below to see how choosing A4 = 440.5 makes notes 49 and below more accurate:

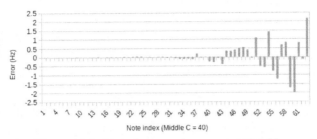

Figure 19.1: Note frequency error at 440.0 Hz

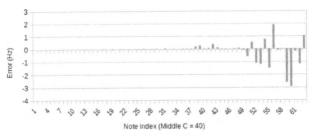

Figure 19.2: Note frequency error at 440.5 Hz

We've provided a Python script `mknotes.py` (see Chapter 30) that figures out the best A4 value for a given range of notes, and then generates a C array containing the Tone Period register values for all the notes. Its first parameter is the highest note for which to optimize, and the second parameter is the number of notes to output. For example:

```
python mknotes.py 49 64
```

19.2 Laying out the Score

Now we just need to list the notes we want to play in order, right?

```
const byte music_score_all_at_once[] = {
  0x2c,0x0d,0x2e,0x2f,0x2e,0x0d,0x2c,0x12 ...
};
```

Not so fast! We also need to know how much time elapses between each note, or each set of notes. If the high bit is set, we decode the byte as a duration. When we hit a duration byte, we pause for the given number of video frames (i.e. *duration*/60 sec) keeping whatever notes are playing.

```
const byte music_score[] = {
      0x2c, // note 44
      0x81, // duration 1
      0x0d, // note 13
      0x8d, // duration 13
      0x2e, // note 46
      0x2f, // note 47
      0x86, // duration 6
      ...
};
```

We only have 3 channels in the AY-3-8910 PSG, so we can only play 3 notes at a time. If we try to play a 4th note while 3 are playing, we'll have to either ignore it, or choose a currently-playing note to interrupt.

19.3 Swinging with the Tempo

First we need to keep track of the three PSG voices. For now, we just need to track the volume for each:

```
struct {
  byte volume;
} voice[3];
```

Every video frame, we'll call `play_music` to update the PSG values. First it sets the volume for each channel, decrementing it each frame to give a "pizzicato" effect:

```
void play_music() {
  byte ch;
  byte enable = 0;     // channel enable flags
  byte freech = 0;     // free channel
  byte chmask = 1;     // this channel's enable flag
  for (ch=0; ch<3; ch++) {
    if (voice[ch].volume) {
      set8910(AY_ENV_VOL_A+ch, voice[ch].volume--);
      enable |= chmask; // enable channel
    } else {
      freech = ch;      // this channel is free
    }
    chmask <<= 1;       // next channel's enable flag
  }
```

19. Making Music

The enable variable tracks currently-playing channels, we'll use this to set the Enable register:

```
set8910(AY_ENABLE, ~enable); // set channel flags
```

We also update freech whenever we see an unused channel, so if we play a new note, we'll know which channel to use.

The next step is to play new notes. If cur_duration is zero, we fetch the next byte from the music data. If it has the high bit set, we update cur_duration. Otherwise, it's a note value, so we look up its value in note_table and set the Tone Period register of the corresponding channel, and also set a new volume in the voice array:

```
if (music_ptr) {
  ch = freech;                            // first free channel
  while (cur_duration == 0) {
    byte note = next_music_byte();        // get next byte
    if ((note & 0x80) == 0) {             // hi bit set == note
      int period = note_table[note & 63]; // set pitch
      set8910(AY_PITCH_A_LO+ch*2, period & 0xff);
      set8910(AY_PITCH_A_HI+ch*2, period >> 8);
      voice[ch].volume = 15;              // set volume
      ch = ch ? ch-1 : 2;                 // use next channel
    } else {
      if (note == 0xff)                   // 0xff = end of song
        music_ptr = NULL;
      cur_duration = note & 63;           // set duration
    }
  }
  cur_duration--;                         // decrement duration
}
```

---

condition ? expr1 : expr2;

If *condition* is true, evaluates *expr1*, otherwise *expr2*.

19.4 Composing the Music

But where does the music data come from? We've created a Python script `midi2song.py` (see Chapter 30) that converts a MIDI file into a music data array. First, pass it a filename to view the MIDI file:

```
$ python midi2song.py morning.mid
```

```
<midi file 'morning.mid' type 1, 13 tracks, 2612 messages>
184.050417521 seconds
Track 0:          (105)  []
Track 1: Words    (165)  []
Track 2: Guitar  (1642)  [1]
Track 3: Flute    (325)  [2]
Track 4: Piano    (317)  [3]
```

You might see just one track, or several tracks. The numbers in [brackets] are the MIDI channels used by each track — sometimes all of the channels are squashed into a single track. To convert a file, pass a comma-separated list of the channels (not the track numbers!) you wish to translate. For this example, we probably want to do channels 1, 2, and 3:

```
$ python midi2song.py morning.mid 1,2,3
```

The script will then parse the MIDI file and output a C array which you can copy and paste into your C source file.

You can also pass a third parameter which transposes the MIDI notes by the desired number of half-steps (negative = down, positive = up).

19.5 Need Some MIDI Files?

The Mutopia Project (mutopiaproject.org) has public domain MIDI files converted from musical scores. The Scott Joplin rags work pretty well for game music.

19.6 Scramble/Frogger Sound Board

These games use a separate sound board with its own Z80 CPU and AY-3-8910 PSGs.[1]

Start	End	Description
$0000	$3FFF	Program ROM
$4000	$43FF	RAM
$6000	$6FFF	Filter network (not emulated)
I/O Port		**Description**
$10		PSG 1: read/write register
$20		PSG 1: select register 0-15
$40		PSG 2: read/write register
$80		PSG 2: select register 0-15

Table 19.1: Scramble/Frogger Sound Board Memory Map

PSG 2 register 14 holds the incoming command from the main CPU. When this value changes, it also triggers a RST 0x38 interrupt.

PSG 2 register 15 is a 1398.2 Hz timer. It has a complex sequence in hardware, but in our emulator, it simply flips between 0 and 255.

---

[1] The 8bitworkshop IDE has some preliminary support for this sound board in the sound_konami platform, although we don't support running it in tandem with the game.

20

Integers and You

Here are a couple of tips for making your integers happy. You'll be happier, and your integers will thank you.

20.1 Powers of Two

For many reasons, computers (and thus computer programmers) really like to work with powers of two. It's a natural thing, since a binary number N bits long can hold N^2 distinct values.

Most C compilers are also aware of the useful properties of binary numbers when dealing with powers of two. For example, we can multiply a number by two by shifting its bits one slot to the left:

```
x <<= 1; // same as x *= 2
```

Shifting left by N bits is the same as multiplying by 2^N:

```
x <<= 2; // same as x *= 4
x <<= 3; // same as x *= 8
```

We can also divide by powers of two (sort of) by shifting to the right:

```
x >>= 1; // same as x /= 2
x >>= 2; // same as x /= 4
```

20. Integers and You

The reason we say "sort of" is because of rounding. For unsigned numbers, division by right shifting rounds the number down towards zero:

```
Binary     Decimal
00001010      9
00000101      5
00000010      2
00000001      1
00000000      0
```

But for signed numbers, the right shift operation uses *sign extension* which keeps the high bit intact during a shift, so that negative numbers stay negative:

```
Binary     Decimal (twos complement)
11110111     -9
11111011     -5
11111101     -3
11111110     -2
11111111     -1
^
|
sign bit
```

This means negative numbers will never be rounded to zero, which is a pretty awful property for a division routine. C compilers are smart enough to optimize multiplication and unsigned division by constant powers of two, sometimes replacing them with equivalent bit shifts. But they won't optimize signed division because of the rounding issue.

For best performance, you should also make the lengths of your array members are powers of two. Primitive types are fine, but if you've defined a struct that is 7 bytes long, consider adding a padding byte to make it 8. The C compiler uses multiplication to compute the address of an array element, and it can optimize powers of two with shifts and/or additions.

The same applies for multi-dimensional arrays – you'll have the best performance with power-of-two dimensions for subarrays.

20.2 Unsigned Comparisons

Consider this: You have a horizontal line that starts at coordinate a and has width w. You need to see if point x intersects the line.

```
        a          a+w
        <---------->
             x
```

Seems pretty easy, right? Here's one way you could do it:

```
char in_range(byte x, byte a, byte w) {
  return x >= a && x <= a+w;
}
```

You could also write it like this:

```
char in_range(byte x, byte a, byte w) {
  return x-a >= 0 && x-a <= w;
}
```

Both of these methods might work, but they are suboptimal. This is because of the C *integer conversion rules*. If 8-bit values are added or subtracted, *integer promotion* converts them to 16-bit values first. The Z80 doesn't have 16-bit instructions for addition, subtraction, or comparison — so the compiled code will be larger.

The following method only requires one comparison, and operates solely on 8-bit values:

```
char in_range(byte x, byte a, byte w) {
  return (byte)(x-a) <= w;
}
```

Note that we cast (x-a) to byte (i.e. unsigned char) before doing the comparison. Since all values are 8-bit quantities, there is no need to promote to 16-bit. Therefore the code generated is a lot smaller.

21

The Atari Vector Hardware

21.1 History

The history of vector games started with the PDP-1 computer and a game called *Spacewar!* developed in 1962 by Steve Russell at MIT. The PDP-1's Type 30 CRT was even more primitive than arcade vector displays, and could only draw individual dots, not lines. Another MIT student, Larry Rosenthal,

Figure 21.1: PDP-1 running Spacewar (By Kenneth Lu, CC BY 2.0)

recreated the game with a homemade CPU and a line-drawing vector display CRT. Cinematronics purchased the technology and released the game as *Space Wars* in 1978.[9]

Atari was not initially interested in Rosenthal's technology, but the next year, they would release a vector game called *Lunar Lander*. It was inspired by an older DEC demo used to promote its vector graphics terminals — itself inspired by a text-based simulation (*LEM*) written in an early interpreted language called FOCAL.

Spacewar! would go on to inspire the hit game *Asteroids*. Atari's Ed Logg used the same basic control scheme for the ship,

21. The Atari Vector Hardware

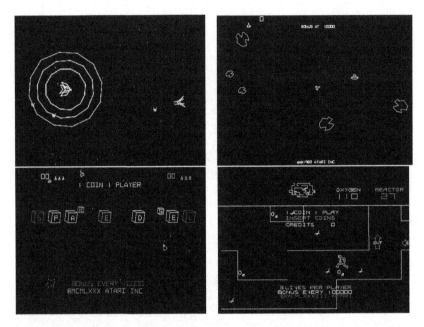

Figure 21.2: Cinematronics' Star Castle, and Atari's Asteroids Deluxe, Space Duel, Major Havoc

including the hyperspace button. Later, Atari would develop RGB color vector technology for the enigmatic *Tempest*, and 3-D wireframe graphics for the arcade version of *Star Wars*.

The unique Vectrex game console brought black-and-white vector graphics to the living room, but by 1985, it was discontinued. Arcade operators were also tired of the fussy and expensive vector monitors, and no new vector games were produced after this year.[1]

21.2 How Vector Monitors Work

The vast majority of arcade monitors were *raster scan* – they swept the electron beam in a regular pattern across the entire frame, like television sets. A *vector monitor*, or "random scan" as it was then called, could direct the electron beam anywhere

---

[1] In 2015, 68 Crew released *VEC9*, a one-of-a-kind arcade game using an old *Asteroids* vector monitor.

on the screen. It could draw precise lines and bright dots on a black background, much like the display on an oscilloscope.

Vector monitors were notoriously finicky and prone to problems. If the electron beam is left stationary too long, the phosphor can "burn in" and leave a spot on the screen — sometimes burning straight through to the glass.[10]

The vector monitors in early black-and-white Atari games were controlled by a custom circuit called a *Digital Vector Generator* (DVG). This circuit is a rudimentary processor which takes instructions from memory and converts them into signals that draw lines on the vector display.

The CPU fills a special area of RAM with DVG instructions (some were also in ROM, used as subroutines) and tells the DVG to start drawing. When the DVG is done, it signals to the CPU that it is ready for the next set of instructions.

The *Analog Vector Generator* (AVG) replaced the DVG in later color games, adding color support, additional scaling effects and simplifying the vector instructions a bit. The AVG is the model we'll use for emulating color games.

21.3 Analog Vector Generator (AVG)

Like a CPU, the AVG fetches opcodes and decodes them to determine which operation to take next. The AVG works with 16-bit words, not 8-bit bytes. The upper 3-4 bits determine the type of operation. The rest of the bits are parameters. (One instruction, VCTR, requires an extra word be fetched.)

The list of AVG commands is as follows:

VCTR

Draws a line from the current beam position to a relative position, defined by an X offset and Y offset added to the current position. The XY offsets are 13-bit signed quantities, so they can range from `-$1000` (-4096) to `$FFF` (4095).

The actual length of the vector on the screen depends on the value passed to the SCAL command, as we'll see next.

21. The Atari Vector Hardware

Opcode	Description	Word Format (MSB-LSB)
VCTR	Draw relative vector.	000YYYYY-YYYYYYYY IIIXXXXX-XXXXXXXX
HALT	Halt	00100000-00000000
SVEC	Draw short relative vector	010YYYYY-IIIXXXXX
STAT	New color/intensity	0110*000-IIII0RGB
SCAL	New scale	0111SSSS-LLLLLLLL
CNTR	Center	10000000-00000000
JSRL	Jump to subroutine	101AAAAA-AAAAAAAA
RTSL	Return from subroutine	11000000-00000000
JMPL	Jump to new address	111AAAAA-AAAAAAAA

```
X     Signed X coordinate offset
Y     Signed Y coordinate offset
RGB   RGB color bits
I     Intensity
L     Linear scale
S     Shift scale
A     Address (word offset, DVG memory)
*     "Sparkle" bit (used in Major Havoc)
```

Table 21.1: List of AVG Commands

An intensity from 0 to 7 is also provided. If is it zero, the beam position is moved, but no line is drawn.

HALT

Halts the AVG and notifies the CPU by setting the VGHALT bit, read through one of the input ports. On a real vector monitor, it's a good idea to center the beam with the CNTR command right before halting.

SVEC

Draws a line from the current position. This command uses a condensed encoding that only uses one word instead of two. This is useful to save memory when drawing complex shapes like text.

The X and Y offsets are provided as signed 5-bit quantities, so they range from -16 to 15. There is also a 3-bit intensity like in VCTR.

The XY offsets are also modified by the SCAL command so the limitation is not as bad as it would seem.

21.3. Analog Vector Generator (AVG)

STAT

Sets a new color and default intensity.

The color is a 3-bit RGB value, for a total of 8 possible colors.

The default intensity is given as a 4-bit value between 0 and 15. This value is substituted whenever the VCTR or SVEC commands specify an intensity of 2.

SCAL

Sets a new scale value. The AVG has two scaling circuits:

Linear (Multiplicitive) scale: A continuous 255-step scaling implemented by analog circuitry. It does not affect the time taken to draw the beam.

Digital (Shift) scale: Directly shifts the bits in the X/Y coordinates before they get to the vector generator. It reduces the time taken to draw the beam.

The actual scale is given by this equation:

$$scale = \frac{(255 - M)^{(8-S)}}{32768}$$

VCTR offsets are multiplied by *scale*; SVEC offsets are multipled by *scale* * 2. The length of the screen on any side is assumed to be 1024.

CNTR

Centers the vector beam. It's a good idea to do this at the beginning and the end of a AVG program.

JSRL

Jumps to a subroutine, given an address.

The AVG has a three-element stack which allows for subroutines. JSRL pushes the next PC onto this stack, then sets the PC to the given address.

21. The Atari Vector Hardware

RTSL

Returns from a subroutine.

This pops a value off the AVG's stack (placed there previously by JSRL) and sets the PC to that value, continuing where it left off.

JMPL

Jumps to an address.

Just like JSRL except it doesn't push anything onto the stack.

21.4 Z80 Memory Map

The original Atari vector games used a 6502 CPU and had varied memory maps for different games.

> For purposes of C programming on the emulator, we're going to create our own hypothetical Z80 architecture. We'll have to tweak the memory map a bit from the original 6502 hardware.
>
> We're also going to substitute the AVG's ROM with RAM to make programming easier, for a total of 16KB of addressable AVG RAM.

Start	End	Description	R/W
$0000	$7FFF	Program ROM	read
$8000	$8003	button inputs	read
$8000	$800F	POKEY 1	write
$8010	$801F	POKEY 2	write
$8100	$810F	Mult Box	r/w
$8840		AVG run until halt	write
$8880		AVG reset	write
$A000	$DFFF	AVG ROM	read
$E000	$FFFF	General-purpose RAM	r/w

Table 21.2: Emulated Z80 Memory Map (vector-z80color)

21.5 AVG C Routines

 To see it on 8bitworkshop.com: Select the **Atari Color Vector (Z80)** platform, then select the **Vector Fonts** file.

First, we declare the 4096 16-bit words that the AVG uses at address $A000:

```
word __at(0xa000) dvgram[0x1000];
```

Our library is going to sequentially write 16-bit words to this array, so we need an index into the array:

```
int dvgwrofs; // write offset for DVG buffer
```

When we want to write a new frame of AVG data, we reset this index with `dvgreset`:

```
inline void dvgreset() {
  dvgwrofs = 0;
}
```

We call `dvgwrite` to write a word to the array:

```
void dvgwrite(word w) {
  dvgram[dvgwrofs++] = w;
}
```

We'll now define a function to write each opcode type. The ones without any parameters are pretty simple:

```
inline void RTSL() {
  dvgwrite(0xc000);
}

inline void CNTR() {
  dvgwrite(0x8000);
}

inline void HALT() {
  dvgwrite(0x2000);
}
```

21. THE ATARI VECTOR HARDWARE

The opcodes with just a single parameter are still pretty simple, we just OR the parameter with the opcode bits:

```
inline void JSRL(word offset) {
  dvgwrite(0xa000 | offset);
}

inline void JMPL(word offset) {
  dvgwrite(0xe000 | offset);
}

inline void SCAL(word scale) {
  dvgwrite(0x7000 | scale);
}
```

The other opcodes that take multiple parameters are pretty complicated, involving a lot of shifting and masking with the AND (&) operator:

```
enum {
  BLACK, BLUE, GREEN, CYAN, RED, MAGENTA, YELLOW, WHITE
} Color;

inline void STAT(byte rgb, byte intens) {
  dvgwrite(0x6000 | ((intens & 0xf)<<4) | (rgb & 7));
}

inline void VCTR(int dx, int dy, byte bright) {
  dvgwrite((dy & 0x1fff));
  dvgwrite(((bright & 7) << 13) | (dx & 0x1fff));
}

inline void SVEC(signed char dx, signed char dy, byte bright) {
  dvgwrite(0x4000 | (dx & 0x1f) | ((bright&7)<<5) | ((dy &
    0x1f)<<8));
}
```

We've even got a function that enables the "sparkling" effect:

```
inline void STAT_sparkle(byte intens) {
  dvgwrite(0x6800 | ((intens & 0xf)<<4));
}
```

21.5. AVG C Routines

To start the AVG and execute the instructions in the list, we call dvgstart:

```
byte __at(0x8840) _dvgstart;

inline void dvgstart() {
  _dvgstart = 0;
}
```

> In our emulator, we don't listen for the AVG's HALT signal — we just assume all vectors are drawn instantaneously.
>
> On actual hardware, you'd likely do some very important calculations while the AVG is running, then wait for the HALT signal before proceeding with the next batch of vectors. Better yet, you could switch between two AVG buffers, filling one while the other is being drawn.

22
3-D Vectors

The first 3D arcade games came out in 1976 — Sega's *Fonz* showed a third-person view of a motorcycle traveling down a road, and Atari's *Night Driver* displayed a minimalist first-person view of road markers at night.

At the 1980 SIGGRAPH conference, Boeing employee Loren Carpenter presented a short film called *Vol Libre*, which depicted a flyby of a computer-generated fractal landscape — later repurposed for the "Genesis Planet" sequence in *Star Trek II: The Wrath of Khan*. (Loren would later co-found Pixar.) This was state-of-the-art at the time, and a two-minute film like this required huge computing resources.

Meanwhile, real-time 3D graphics in games was just getting started. Home computers were running subLOGIC's *Flight Simulator*. Atari's *Battlezone* and *Red Baron* were making waves in arcades with their 3D vector graphics technology.

> ▸ To see it on 8bitworkshop.com: Select the **Atari Color Vector (Z80)** platform, then select the **3D Transformations** file.

22.1 3D Types

We don't have floating point hardware (we could emulate it in software, but it'd be so slow as to be unplayable), so we use fixed-point integer types for everything.

22. 3-D Vectors

Figure 22.1: Frame from Loren C. Carpenter's "Vol Libre"

We define 3D coordinates with X, Y, and Z values, and we need both 8-bit and 16-bit 3D vectors (i.e., a coordinate — the mathematical kind of vector, not the vector-graphics kind of vector):

```
typedef struct {
  sbyte x,y,z;
} Vector8; // 8-bit signed XYZ vector

typedef struct {
  int x,y,z;
} Vector16; // 16-bit signed XYZ vector
```

In 3D graphics, the orientation (rotation) of an object can be stored in a 3x3 matrix. We only need 8-bit precision for our purposes, so we define a 3x3 array of signed bytes:

```
typedef struct {
  sbyte m[3][3];
} Matrix;
```

Matrix coefficients range from -127 to 127. The most basic kind of matrix is the *identity matrix*, which leaves its input vector unchanged:

$$\begin{bmatrix} 1 & 0 & 0 \\ 0 & 1 & 0 \\ 0 & 0 & 1 \end{bmatrix}$$

This is how it would be set in C:

```
void mat_identity(Matrix* m) {
  memset(m, 0, sizeof(*m));
  m->m[0][0] = 127;
  m->m[1][1] = 127;
  m->m[2][2] = 127;
}
```

To do anything useful, though, we have to compute the sine and cosine functions.

22.2 Sine and Cosine

We used a 32-entry sine table way back in Chapter 18. We need more accuracy for this application, so we're going to encode our angles in an entire byte (256 values):

Byte	Degrees	Radians
0	0 deg	0/256 PI
64	90 deg	64*2/256 PI
128	180 deg	128*2/256 PI
192	270 deg	192*2/256 PI

22. 3-D Vectors

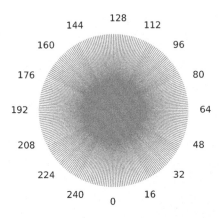

Figure 22.2: Compass directions of 256-byte sine table

Because of trigonometric symmetries, we only need a 64-entry lookup table for 256 distinct angles:

```
const sbyte sintbl[64] = {
0, 3, 6, 9, 12, 16, 19, 22, 25, 28, 31, 34, 37, 40, 43, 46,
49, 51, 54, 57, 60, 63, 65, 68, 71, 73, 76, 78, 81, 83, 85, 88,
90, 92, 94, 96, 98, 100, 102, 104, 106, 107, 109, 111, 112,
    113, 115, 116,
117, 118, 120, 121, 122, 122, 123, 124, 125, 125, 126, 126,
    126, 127, 127, 127,
};
```

---

switch (index) {
case constantA: statementA; **break;**
case constantB: statementB; **break;**
...
default: default-statement; **break;**
}

A *switch statement*. Evaluates *index*, comparing it against each *case* constant and executing the corresponding statement if a match is found. If no match is found, executes *default-statement*.

22.3. Wireframe Models

For each quadrant (90-degree range) of the angle we can compute a different expression:

```
sbyte isin(byte x) {
  switch (x>>6) {
    case 0: return sintbl[x];
    case 1: return sintbl[127-x];
    case 2: return -sintbl[x-128];
    case 3: return -sintbl[255-x];
  }
}
```

With some clever bit testing, we can optimize this routine further, reducing its compiled size from 103 bytes to 43 bytes:

```
sbyte isin(byte x0) {
  byte x = x0;
  if (x0 & 0x40) x = 127-x;
  if (x0 & 0x80) {
    return -sintbl[x+128];
  } else {
    return sintbl[x];
  }
}
```

22.3 Wireframe Models

Our shapes will be *wireframe models* — points connected by lines. They consist of a number of *vertices*, or 3D points, connected by a number of *edges*, or lines between vertices.

```
typedef struct {
  byte numverts;
  const Vector8* verts; // array of vertices
  const sbyte* edges;   // array of vertex indices (edges)
} Wireframe;
```

We represent the edges as a list of vertex indices, with two special values. When we want to turn the beam off, we use a value of -1 — the beam will start drawing with the next vertex index. A -2 marks the end of the list.

22. 3-D Vectors

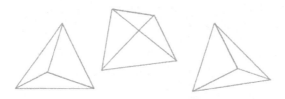

Figure 22.3: Rotations of a tetrahedron

We're going to use *initializers* to define the various parts of our Wireframe object in ROM. The following defines a simple tetrahedron (a triangular pyramid) with four vertices and six edges:

```
const Vector8 tetra_v[] = {
    {0,-86,86},{86,86,86},{-86,86,86},{0,0,-86} };
const char tetra_e[] = { 0, 1, 2, 0, 3, 1, -1, 3, 2, -2 };
const Wireframe tetra = { 4, tetra_v, tetra_e };
```

This is how you define complex objects in C. For tetra_e, we use an *array initializer* which defines an array of chars (signed bytes) but does not specify a length; the compiler takes up only as much space as is needed.

For tetra_v, we define an array of *struct initializers*, which is why the {} brackets are nested. For example, {0,-86,86} defines the x, y, and z fields of a single Vector8 struct in the array.

Note also the const keyword which tells the compiler to put the definitions in ROM.

22.4 Transformation

To rotate a 3D coordinate using a matrix, we use the following function:

```
void vec_mat_transform2(Vector16* dest, const Vector8* v,
    const Matrix* m) {
  dest->x = v->x*m->m[0][0] + v->y*m->m[0][1] +
    v->z*m->m[0][2];
  dest->y = v->x*m->m[1][0] + v->y*m->m[1][1] +
    v->z*m->m[1][2];
  dest->z = v->x*m->m[2][0] + v->y*m->m[2][1] +
    v->z*m->m[2][2];
}
```

We'll only use 3D coordinate values ranging from -86 to 86. Why? To avoid overflow when doing calculations. For a 3D transform, we must compute the sum of three multiplications for each coordinate. Our matrix coefficients go up to 127, so 86 is the maximum value we can have for our matrix until they overflow the 16-bit signed integer. (127*86*3 = 32766 < 32767)

Our matrix transform function is a pretty slow and bloated routine. We can do a lot better using our custom emulated math hardware, which we'll describe next.

22.5 The Mult Box

The 6502 CPU does not have multiply or divide instructions, which had to be emulated with software routines — this is very slow.

To speed up 3D calculations, Atari vector games (starting with *Battlezone* and *Red Baron*) used a custom circuit called the "Math Box," built around four AMD 2901 bitslice processors.[1] It could perform 16-bit multiplications, additions, and divisions much faster than the Z80 CPU.

---
[1] The hard-wired CPU in Cinematronics games also used these chips.

22. 3-D Vectors

Our emulator does not model the Math Box precisely, but it's got something similar which we've designed to be easy-to-use. We'll call it "The Mult Box," and it has these addresses:

$8100-$8101	16-bit sum
$8102	8-bit multiplicand A
$8103	8-bit multiplicand B
$8104-$8105	16-bit dividend (sum / A)
$810F	compute sum += A * B (strobe)

To do a sum-of-products, first set the 16-bit value at $8100 to 0. For each product, set $8102 to the first multiplicand and $8103 to the second multiplicand, then strobe $810F. The multiplication will commence and the product will be added to the 16-bit sum. When finished, read the 16-bit sum at $8100.

The Mult Box also divides. Before we update sum, it computes the 16-bit dividend *sum/A* and stores it at $8104.

Using the Mult Box, our matrix transformation looks like this:

```
inline void mul16(sbyte a, sbyte b) {
  mathbox_arg1 = a;
  mathbox_arg2 = b;
  mathbox_go_mul=0; // mathbox_sum += a * b
}

void vec_mat_transform(Vector16* dest, const Vector8* v, const
    Matrix* m) {
  byte i;
  // compute a pointer to the first element of our destination
  // vector, and a pointer to the first element of the matrix.
  int* result = &dest->x;
  const signed char* mval = &m->m[0][0];
  // loop over all 3 vector elements (x, y, z)
  for (i=0; i<3; i++) {
    mathbox_sum = 0;           // reset sum to 0
    mul16(*mval++, v->x);
    mul16(*mval++, v->y);
    mul16(*mval++, v->z);
    *result++ = mathbox_sum;   // fetch final sum, store
  }
}
```

162

23

Game: Crowded Orbit

Now we're going to take what we've learned about vector graphics and 3D transformations and make an actual game. You're the captain of a ship in a very crowded orbit, and you have to get rid of space junk by blasting it, and avoid getting smashed by it.

> ▶ To see it on 8bitworkshop.com: Select the **Atari Color Vector (Z80)** platform, then select the **Space Game** file.

23.1 Shape Prerendering

Drawing individual vectors takes a lot of CPU time, especially when rotations and 3D transformations are involved, so we're going to speed things up by *prerendering*.

Figure 23.1: Our game for this chapter, "Crowded Orbit"

23. Game: Crowded Orbit

In most vector games, the prerendering was done offline by a "real" computer and baked into the ROM. The prerendering software could be pretty advanced, for instance performing *hidden line removal* which could take hours. Sometimes shapes were even edited by hand!

We're going to perform the prerendering in RAM, when our program starts. For each shape, we're going to choose a limited set of rotations and put the drawing instructions into RAM. When we need to draw the shape at a certain angle, we look up the prerendered shape's address in memory and use the JSRL opcode to draw it.

It's not as difficult as it seems. First we choose the AVG offset where our prerendered shapes will start:

```
dvgwrofs = 0x800; // AVG offset of prerendered shapes region
```

We declare a global buffer for each shape, and choose how many rotations we'll prerender — 32 is a good number:

```
word ship_shapes[32];
word thrust_shapes[32];
word tetra_shapes[32];
```

Prerendering is the same as drawing: compute the transformation matrix, then output the drawing instructions. The only difference is a RTSL opcode at the end, since these are subroutines meant to be used by the JSRL command:

```
void make_cached_shapes() {
  Matrix mat;
  byte i;
  for (i=0; i<32; i++) {
    ship_shapes[i] = dvgwrofs; // start of shape
    mat_rotate(&mat, 2, i<<3); // 32<<3 == 32*8 == 256
    draw_wireframe_ortho(&ship_wf, &mat);
    RTSL(); // end of shape
    // ...draw other shapes...
  }
}
```

23.2 Actors

To make things easier, we're going to define a type which holds the data for all moveable objects on the screen. We'll call this an Actor, and we'll define it with a struct:

```
typedef struct Actor {
  word* shapes;              // array of AVG offsets
  ActorUpdateFn* update_fn;  // update function
  byte angshift;             // converts angle to shape
    index
  byte scale;                // scale
  byte color;                // color
  byte intens;               // intensity
  byte collision_flags;      // collision compatibility
  byte angle;                // angle (0-255)
  word xx;                   // fixed-point X
  word yy;                   // fixed-point Y
  int velx;                  // X velocity
  int vely;                  // Y velocity
  struct Actor* next;        // next actor in linked list
  byte removed:1;            // 'removed' flag
} Actor;
```

Note that we put the keyword Actor both before and after the curly brackets. This is because of the way C defines *namespaces*. A namespace is a bucket that holds unique identifiers.

We've mainly used the *global namespace* up until this point, which includes function names, typedefs, global variable names, etc. The Actor identifier after the } goes in the global namespace.

There is also a *tag namespace* which holds identifiers for struct names. The identifier after the struct keyword but before the { goes into the tag namespace. We can use the same identifier, Actor, in both places because they are separate namespaces.

Why use the tag namespace anyway? We need it if we want to refer to the struct type within its own definition. For example, the next pointer is of type struct Actor:

```
struct Actor* next;
```

The `Actor` in the struct namespace has been defined, but the `Actor` in the global namespace hasn't yet. But both identifiers refer to the same struct definition, so they're interchangable.

It's also a good idea to declare the struct as an incomplete type before the struct is defined. If you need to use the struct name as part of other typedefs, this will prevent "incompatible type" errors:

```
typedef struct Actor;           // incomplete type
// ...other typedefs go here...
typedef struct Actor {          // complete type
  // define fields ...
```

23.3 Drawing Actors

Drawing an actor requires several instructions. First we center the beam in the middle of the screen:

```
CNTR();
```

Now we change to *screen scale* so we can move the beam to the center of the actor. The value $2C0 covers pretty much the entire screen:

```
SCAL(0x2c0); // screen scale
```

Then we move the beam to the actor's center. The actor's X/Y coordinates are 16-bit, but we only have 13 bits of precision in the VCTR command, so we shift each coordinate right by 3 bits (16-3 == 13):

```
VCTR(a->xx >> 3, a->yy >> 3, 0); // actor center
```

Now we convert to *object scale* to draw the actor. Having two separate scales lets us make individual actors larger and smaller:

```
SCAL(a->scale); // object scale
```

Each actor also has its own color and intensity:

```
STAT(a->color, a->intens);
```

Now we draw the shape, based on the actor's current angle. The `angshift` member is set based on how many shapes are prerendered – for example, for 32 shapes you'd have an `angshift` of 3 (256 >> 3 == 32). Then simply extract the correct shape's address from the `shapes` array and output the JSRL (Jump to Subroutine) opcode:

```
JSRL(a->shapes[a->angle >> a->angshift]);
```

23.4 Moving Actors

Our game follows the law of inertia — an object in motion remains in motion until a force is applied. We keep the current fixed-point velocity of an actor in `velx` and `vely`, and update the posiiton every frame by adding the velocity to each component:

```
void move_actor(Actor* a) {
  a->xx += a->velx;
  a->yy += a->vely;
}
```

`xx` and `yy` are `int`s, so they wrap around at `$7FFF` (32767) and -`$8000` (-32768).

To apply thrust to the player's ship, we compute the sin and cosine of the ship's angle, then add them to a player's velocity:

```
void thrust_ship() {
  sbyte sin = isin(curship->angle);
  sbyte cos = icos(curship->angle);
  curship->velx += sin>>3; // divide by 8
  curship->vely += cos>>3; // divide by 8
}
```

Additionally, the player's ship has a friction force so that it eventually drifts to a stop when thrust is released. This also gives it a maximum velocity. We apply to each velocity component an inverse force proportional to itself:

```
int apply_friction(int vel) {
  int delta = vel >> 8;         // divide by 256
  if (delta == 0 && vel > 0)
    delta++;                    // make sure force is nonzero
  return vel - delta;           // subtract force
}
```

We've ensured that the force along an axis is nonzero as long as the velocity component is nonzero, so that the ship eventually stops. This may make the ship tend to slide along the X or Y axis as it comes to a halt, since one component will usually get zeroed out before the other.

23.5 Allocating Memory with malloc()

Up until now, we've kept game objects in fixed-size arrays in global memory. For this game, we're going to keep our actors in *dynamic memory*, or the *heap* — and access them via a data structure called a *linked list*.

First, let's talk about *memory allocation*. We've seen two types of allocation: *static allocation* (*global variables*) and *stack allocation* (*local variables*). For both types, the compiler takes care of allocation and deallocation — in the case of global variables, they are simply reserved a slot in memory.

We can allocate a fixed number of bytes in the *heap* using malloc, passing the size of the object:

```
malloc(sizeof(Actor))
```

The malloc function returns a pointer to the allocated memory block, or NULL if the allocation failed due to lack of heap space. To use the returned pointer, we do something like this:

```
Actor* a = (Actor*) malloc(sizeof(Actor));
```

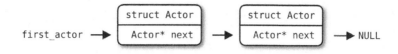

Figure 23.2: Linked list data structure

The (Actor*) expression is a *type cast* – it converts the *untyped* (void*) pointer to a typed (Actor*) pointer, since we intend to use the allocated memory as an Actor struct.

When we no longer need the allocated memory, we simply call free on the pointer returned by malloc:

```
free(a);
```

When using malloc and free, there are a couple of gotchas to watch out for:

- *Running out of memory*: The C library allocates a finite portion of memory, called the *heap*, to dynamic allocation. In our system, this is whatever RAM is left over after the global variables are declared. Because the stack lives at the top end of RAM, you may get stack corruption before you actually run out of memory.
- *Dangling pointers*: You might free() an object while still having pointers pointing to it. This generally causes problems, especially when the freed object's space is reused by other objects.

23.6 Linked Lists

If we plan to have a large list of objects that grows and shrinks dynamically, we might want to use a *linked list*.

A linked list is a chain of objects that are linked by pointers. Each object points to the next one in line, and the last object points to NULL. (A NULL pointer is a special value that denotes "nothing pointed to," and it's usually got the value of 0. Make sure there's nothing you want to point to at address 0x0!)

23. Game: Crowded Orbit

To iterate through all objects in the linked list: Start with a pointer to the first object (this is kept separately) then follow the "next" pointers in each object until you get a NULL. You'll visit every object in the list.

We can do this to draw all actors, for example:

```
Actor* a = first_actor;
while (a != NULL) {
  draw_actor(a);       // draw actor
  a = a->next;         // move pointer to next actor
}
```

To create a new actor and add it to the list, we have to do a couple of things. First, we allocate memory for the new actor, and get a pointer to it. Then, we set whichever fields need setting, and set its next pointer. We then change the first_actor pointer so that it's at the head of the list:

```
Actor* new_actor(const Actor* base) {
  Actor* a = (Actor*) malloc(sizeof(Actor)); // allocate
  memcpy(a, base, sizeof(Actor));  // copy starting values
  a->next = first_actor;           // set a's next pointer
  first_actor = a;                 // set head of list ptr.
  return a;
}
```

We pass to new_actor a base pointer that points to an example (prototype) object, so that we can easily fill in some default data for the new actor, like its shape, scale, color, etc. We declare the base actor with a *struct initializer*, which we briefly saw in the previous chapter:

```
const Actor ship_actor = {
  ship_shapes, NULL, 3, 0xb0, WHITE, 7, 0x1
};
```

This constructs an Actor struct in ROM with some fields pre-filled with our initialized values. We have to put them in the same order as the struct declaration — if we don't put enough values for all of them, the remainder of the struct will be set to zero bytes.

23.7 Function Pointers

Function pointers are variables that store the address of a function. You call a function pointer just like a function, passing it parameters and returning its result. The function pointer will call the underlying function at its address, which may be one of several different underlying functions.

We'd like our actors to not only have their own shape and appearance, but their own behavior. We can add a function pointer to the Actor definition to give it this ability:

```
ActorUpdateFn* update_fn;
```

ActorUpdateFn is a *function type*, and so ActorUpdateFn* is a pointer to a function. The function type is declared with a typedef:

```
typedef void ActorUpdateFn(struct Actor*);
```

This tells the compiler that our function type ActorUpdateFn takes a pointer to an Actor and returns void (nothing). Any function with the same *function signature* will be compatible – in other words, with the same number and type of parameters and the same return type.

Note that our parameter is of type struct Actor* instead of Actor*. This is because we've got to declare the function type before the Actor struct is defined, and so we need to declare Actor as an *incomplete type*:

```
struct Actor;
```

This tells the compiler that there is a struct called Actor so we can use it in declarations. We don't know its size or what data members it has yet, so if we tried to do anything else besides make pointer types with it, we'd probably cause a compiler error. (It's an *incomplete type,* just like void.)

23.8 Deleting Objects

Eventually, objects will be destroyed and we'll have to remove them from the list of actors. Removing items from a linked list is a little tricky, for a number of reasons:

1. The next pointers have to be rewritten so that the object to be deleted is skipped in the chain.

2. The same goes for the first_actor pointer (the first item in the list).

3. It gets complicated if an object is deleted while a list is being iterated over.

4. Memory must be freed.

We're going to set a removed flag in the Actor object so that we can defer its removal from the linked list until later.

After we update all objects, we run through the list again to check for the removed flag. We keep a pointer to another pointer (the C type is Actor **) so that we can rewrite the previous pointer when needed:

```
Actor** prev = &first_actor;
```

We can grab the Actor pointer from this pointer:

```
while (a = *prev) {
```

If the object was removed, we set the previous pointer to this object's next pointer — skipping the deleted object:

```
if (a->removed) {
  // set previous pointer to skip this actor
  *prev = a->next;
  // free memory
  free(a);
```

Otherwise, we grab the address of the next pointer, which becomes our new prev:

```
} else {
  prev = &a->next;
}
```

23.9 Collision Detection

It'd be nice if the hardware could detect when two vectors cross. Unfortunately, it can't. So we still have to do everything in software.

Instead of doing things on a vector-by-vector basis, we're going to test actors against each other. We'll have to iterate through every pair of actors that could potentially collide, comparing their positions to see if they overlap.

Collision detection routines often use a simple test to see if an object should be considered before moving on to more complex tests. A *bounding box* test is a common test because it's computationally simple. This puts a generous rectangle around each actor, and we'll only consider two actors for further collision testing if their bounding boxes intersect.

We're going to use a *radius test* in our collision detector, because all of our moving objects are (approximately) round. The rule is: If the distance between the centers of a pair of objects is smaller than the sum of their radii, then they are assumed to collide.

How do we calculate the distance? If you remember your trigonometry, the formula for the length of the side of a right triangle is $\sqrt{x^2 + y^2}$. We can compare that against our minimum collision distance *mindist*.

However, square roots take a lot of CPU cycles to compute. Instead, we'll square both terms: We'll use the squared distance $(x^2 + y^2)$ and compare it against $mindist^2$.

Because even multiplication is expensive on our 8-bit CPU, we'll do an initial test before computing the distance, using the *Manhattan distance* – which is just $(x + y)$. This value will always be greater or equal to the actual distance, so we can use it to filter out candidates.

There is also a `collision_flags` field for each actor which we can use to filter out candidates based on type. For example, one flag is set for the player's ship, one for player torpedoes, and one for obstacles. We pass the set of flags that we're looking for, and the routine only considers collisions against objects that have any matching flags.

Our main collision routine looks like this:

```
if ((a->collision_flags & flags) && !a->removed) {
  byte dx = abs(xx1 - (a->xx >> 8)); // abs(x1-x2)
  byte dy = abs(yy1 - (a->yy >> 8)); // abs(y1-y2)
  if (dx+dy < mindist) { // check Manhattan distance
    word dist2 = get_distance_squared(dx, dy);
    if (dist2 < mindist2) { // d^2 < mindist^2?
      if (fn) fn(actl, a);    // call hit function
      count++;                // inc. hit counter
    }
  }
}
```

The `get_distance_squared` function uses our hardware multiplier to compute $(x^2 + y^2)$:

```
inline word get_distance_squared(byte dx, byte dy) {
  mathbox_sum = 0;
  mul16(dx,dx);
  mul16(dy,dy);
  return mathbox_sum; // dx^2 + dy^2
}
```

Note that we first convert coordinates from 16-bit fixed-point to 8-bit integer (i.e., shifted right by 8) so that we don't overflow when multiplying.

23.10 The Main Loop

First, we fill the DVG RAM with 0x20 (HALT) opcodes in case we mess something up and the DVG goes into the weeds:

```
memset(dvgram, 0x20, sizeof(dvgram)); // HALTs
```

Now, we make our cached shapes. We set the DVG write offset to $800 and call the routines:

```
dvgwrofs = 0x800;
make_cached_font();
make_cached_shapes();
```

23.10. The Main Loop

Then we create our game objects, the obstacles, and the player ship:

```
create_obstacles(5);
new_player_ship();
```

Now our main game loop starts. We'll loop until there is exactly one actor in the actor list, which means we've cleared all of the obstacles and only the player's ship remains (and there are no more explosions, torpedoes, etc.):

```
while (!just_one_actor_left()) {
```

This function is pretty simple:

```
byte just_one_actor_left() {
  return first_actor && first_actor->next == NULL;
}
```

This function also demonstrates *short-circuit evaluation* of logical operators like && and || in C. Logical expressions are evaluated left-to-right, and if the left part is false, the right part is never evaluated at all. This is why we check first_actor on the left side — to protect the right side from potentially evaluating a null pointer and crashing the program (it wouldn't crash on a Z80, because there's no memory protection, but you'd get a nonsensical result).

In our main loop, we first reset the DVG write pointer to start a new vector program. We then call control_player to read the player's inputs and control the ship, then draw_and_update_actors to draw, move, and process all of the actors:

```
dvgreset();
control_player();
draw_and_update_actors();
```

23. Game: Crowded Orbit

Now we do a CNTR to center the vector beam before we write our final HALT instruction — a good practice to avoid stressing out the virtual magnets in the virtual CRT. Then we call `dvgstart` to tell the DVG to start processing vectors:

```
CNTR();
HALT();
dvgstart();
```

While we're waiting for the DVG, we remove any actors that got flagged as "removed" in the update step:

```
remove_expired_actors();
```

Then we update the `frame` counter and pet the watchdog:

```
frame++;
watchdog = 0;
```

Since our loop takes a variable number of CPU cycles depending on the number of objects, we need a way to keep our video frame rate consistent. There's no VSYNC signal in a vector monitor, but in our emulator, we've added a simple hardware counter (`vidframe`) that increments every 1/60 second, counting from 0 to 3 and wrapping back to 0.

We already have an internal counter, `frame`, so to limit our frame rate we just spin the CPU as long as the first two bits of `frame` are equal to the hardware counter (`vidframe`):

```
while (vidframe == (frame & 0x3)) {}
```

As long as the game loop takes less than 1/60 second, the loop will stay in sync with the counter. But if our loop ever takes longer than that, the counter will go out of sync and take four iterations to catch up again. (This is similar to how we did it in Chapter 18.)

24

The POKEY Sound Chip

The POKEY (POtentiometer and KEYboard) is a proprietary sound and interface chip, first featured in the Atari home computers and the *Battlezone* and *Asteroids Deluxe* arcade games. Atari manufactured three versions of the chip, a single-core version for home computers and consoles, and dual-core and quad-core POKEYs for arcade games.

The POKEY chip was designed by Doug Neubauer, who also proved his software skills with Atari's futuristic 3D space combat game *Star Raiders*. POKEY's sound generator is an upgraded version of the one found on the Atari VCS/2600. Besides making sound, it could read paddle controllers and keyboards, handle serial communications, and generate random numbers.

Figure 24.1: POKEY chip (by RodCastler, CC BY-SA 3.0)

24. The POKEY Sound Chip

24.1 Memory Map

Offset	Name	Description
$00	AUDF1	Channel 1 Frequency
$01	AUDC1	Channel 1 Control
$02	AUDF2	Channel 2 Frequency
$03	AUDC2	Channel 2 Control
$04	AUDF3	Channel 3 Frequency
$05	AUDC3	Channel 3 Control
$06	AUDF4	Channel 4 Frequency
$07	AUDC4	Channel 4 Control
$08	AUDCTL	Audio Control
$0A	RANDOM	Random Number (read-only)

24.2 AUDCTL Bit Map

The AUDCTL register configures global settings of the POKEY:

Bit #	Description
0	Clock base (0=64 kHz, 1=15 kHz)
1	Channel 2/4 high-pass filter
2	Channel 1/3 high-pass filter
3	Sync channels 4/3
4	Sync channels 2/1
5	Channel 3 clock 1.79 MHz
6	Channel 1 clock 1.79 MHz
7	Use 9-bit poly counter

The POKEY works by dividing the frequency of a common clock, just like the AY-3-8910 we covered in Chapter 9. Whereas the 8910 has 12-bit divisors, the POKEY has selectable 8-bit or 16-bit divisors. The 16-bit divisors are helpful for accurate musical pitches, and are configured by pairing two 8-bit channels.

24.3 AUDCx Bit Map

Each of the 4 channels has its own AUDC register. The lower nibble of the AUDC register sets the 4-bit volume of the channel.

24.4. Setting AUDF Frequency

The upper nibble selects the polynomial, which controls the output waveform.

Hex	Bit # 76543210	Description	Period
xV	xxxx	Volume (0-15, 0=off)	
0x	0000....	17-bit poly * 5-bit poly	noise
2x	0010....	5-bit poly	31
4x	0100....	4-bit poly * 5-bit poly	31
6x	0110....	5-bit poly	31
8x	1000....	17-bit poly	noise
Ax	1010....	pure tone	2
Cx	1100....	4-bit poly	15
1x	xxx1....	Waveform mode	

24.4 Setting AUDF Frequency

When using a pure tone, the output frequency of each channel depends on the bits set in AUDCTL:

Frequency	Condition
64 kHz	AUDCTL bit 0 clear
15 kHz	AUDCTL bit 0 set
1.79 MHz	AUDCTL bit 6 set (ch1) or bit 5 (ch3)

The period of each polynomial roughly determines the audible frequency of the tone, lower periods having higher frequency.

When $Fclock$ is 64000 Hz or 15000 Hz, the output frequency $Fout$ is given by this equation:

$$Frequency = \frac{Clock}{PolyPeriod \cdot (AUDF + 4)}$$

When using the 1.79 MHz clock:

$$Frequency = \frac{1790000}{PolyPeriod \cdot (AUDF + 1)}$$

24. The POKEY Sound Chip

If channels 1 and 2 are synced (with AUDCTL bit 4) then the output frequency for both channels is:

$$Frequency = \frac{Clock}{PolyPeriod \cdot (AUDF2 * 256 + AUDF1 + 7)}$$

If channels 3 and 4 are synced then the output frequency is:

$$Frequency = \frac{Clock}{PolyPeriod \cdot (AUDF4 * 256 + AUDF3 + 7)}$$

24.5 POKEY Music

By using two POKEYs and putting both pairs of channels into 16-bit mode, you can play high-accuracy musical tones. The technique is similar to that in Chapter 19.

> 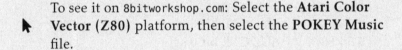 To see it on 8bitworkshop.com: Select the **Atari Color Vector (Z80)** platform, then select the **POKEY Music** file.

25

Miscellaneous C Topics

There are a couple of advanced C topics we haven't covered yet, so we'll talk about them here.

25.1 Unions

In the upcoming chapters, you may see the following inside of a type definition:

```
union {
  struct { sbyte dx,dy; } laser;      // laser direction
  struct { byte exploding; } enemy;   // enemy exploding
} u;
```

This is called a *union* type, and it's similar to a struct except instead of its fields being contiguous in memory, all of its fields overlap in memory. This conserves space for fields that don't need to coexist.

In the above example, lasers have a direction, and enemies explode, but we don't have objects that need both attributes at the same time. So we define a struct for each object type and put them both in a union.

There is no check to see if you are using the union properly, so you could, for example, write to the laser struct and read from the enemy struct. But you probably shouldn't.

25. Miscellaneous C Topics

25.2 Big Numbers

You can define a *floating-point* value with the `float` type:

```
float floatval = 123.45;
```

They are stored as IEEE single-precision floats, which take up 4 bytes of memory and range from -10^{38} to 10^{38}. They only have 23 bits of precision, and are very slow to compute on 8-bit platforms, so they are not very useful for 8-bit games.

The `long` type defines a 4 byte (32-bit) integer type which can range from 0 to $2^{32} - 1$ (unsigned). All of the examples in this book get along just fine with 16-bit numbers — they're faster and use less memory.

25.3 Advanced Loop Handling

We covered the `break` keyword, which exits a loop, in Chapter 7. There is also a `continue` keyword which restarts the loop. It can be used in `for` and `while` statements. For example:

```
for (i=0; i<100; i++) {
  // enemy sleeping? ignore them
  if (enemy[i].is_sleeping) continue;
  // ... process rest of enemy ...
}
```

There is also a `goto` statement that jumps to a label defined elsewhere in your program. This is useful for breaking out of multiple nested loops, for example:

```
  for (i=0; i<10; i++) {
    for (j=0; j<10; j++) {
      if (grid[i][j]) goto breakout; // break out of loop
    }
  }
  // this only executes if we didn't break out of the loop
  not_found();
breakout: // this is a label
  // continue executing here
```

25.4 Operator Precedence

Grade-school children learn about the *operator precedence* of addition versus multiplication — for example, multiplication takes precedence over addition, so 1+2*3 = 1+(2*3).

C has a *whole bunch* of operator precedence rules, which are often learned through making mistakes. There are also *operator associativity* rules, which determines if expressions are grouped from right-to-left or left-to-right.

Here's an almost-complete list of operators, with highest precedence at the top and lowest at the bottom:

f() a[] a.b a->b x++	Primary operators	left-to-right
++x !x ~x (type) *p &o	Unary operators	right-to-left
* / %	Multiply/divide/mod	left-to-right
+ -	Add/subtract	left-to-right
« »	Shift	left-to-right
< <= > >=	Relational	left-to-right
== !=	Equality	left-to-right
& ^ |	Bitwise	left-to-right
&& ^^ ||	Logical	left-to-right
? :	Conditional	right-to-left
= += -= etc.	Assignment	right-to-left
,	Comma operator	left-to-right

Some general tips:

- When in doubt, use parenthesis.
- Be especially careful when mixing bit operations with comparisons. `a & b == 1` is parsed as `a & (b == 1)` which is probably not what you intended.

26

Williams Hardware

26.1 History

Eugene Jarvis quit Hewlett-Packard to make pinball games for Atari, then Williams Electronics hired him to make sound for pinball machines. He used a Motorola 6800 CPU to make strange noises with an 8-bit digital-analog converter (DAC). He would then become lead designer for Williams' first video game, called *Defender*.[11]

The Williams hardware team designed an elegant architecture that left most of the power (and responsibility) in the software developers' hands. *Defender* uses a frame buffer — like *Space Invaders* — but in full color. The frame buffer is 304 by 256 pixels with 4 bits (16 colors) per pixel, taking up 36 KB of memory — in 1980, that was a lot. Each of the 16 colors can be chosen from a 256-color RGB palette.

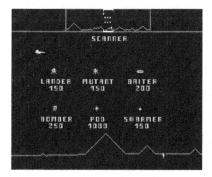 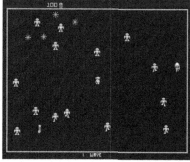

Figure 26.1: Williams' Defender, Robotron

Lacking any sort of hardware acceleration, the Defender developers achieved its lightning speed by using pixel-sparse visuals and clever tricks. For games like *Joust* and *Robotron*, Greg Wepner created a custom *bit blitter* chip.[12] This was a powerful 4 MHz coprocessor that could draw sprites and rectangles to the frame buffer at astounding speeds for the time — moving almost 1 MB/sec of data. This gave games like *Robotron: 2084* their massive sprite count. Called "the Special Chips," they worked as a pair, each chip handling 4 bits at a time (a single pixel).[13]

Defender was one of the first video games to use the Motorola 6809 CPU. Many Williams games were written on a Motorola EXORciser, an early desktop computer that could assemble 6800 and 6809 programs.[14]

> We've adapted the emulator to run the Williams architecture with the Z80. It runs the CPU at 4 MHz, a speed available on the Z80A chips available in 1981.

26.2 Memory Map

Start	End	Description	R/W
$0000	$97FF	bankswitched (video RAM, program ROM)	r/w
$9800	$BFFF	general-purpose RAM	r/w
$C000	$C00F	video palette	write
$C804	$C807	control inputs	read
$C80C	$C80F	control inputs	read
$C900	$C9FF	bank select	write
$CA00	$CA07	bit blitter	write
$CB00		video counter	read
$CBFF		watchdog	write
$CC00	$CFFF	NVRAM (diagnostics, high scores)	r/w
$D000	$FFFF	ROM	read

Table 26.1: Wililams (Stargate/Robotron/Joust) Memory Map

26.3 Bankswitched RAM/ROM

The video frame buffer is so large that there's not much room left in the 16-bit address space for ROM access. So, the RAM and ROM coexist at $0000-$97FF via bank-switching. Writes always go to RAM, but reads can come from either RAM or ROM depending on the value of the bank-switching bit at $C900.

While reading from video RAM, the CPU's program counter must be within the upper ROM space ($D000-$FFFF), otherwise the CPU will try to execute code in the video frame buffer!

Reading from video memory is infrequent, but can be useful for buffer-to-buffer copying and certain collision detection routines.

26.4 Video Frame Buffer

 To see it on 8bitworkshop.com: Select the **Williams (Z80)** platform, then select the **Graphics Test** file.

The Williams games' frame buffer is atypical; although the monitor is mounted horizontally[1], and thus scanlines are horizontal, consecutive bytes in memory go downward on the screen.

Each byte contains two pixels — the upper four bits on the left, and the lower four bits on the right. Each 4-bit pixel is mapped to the 16-color palette.

It's defined in C as a 152 x 256 byte array:

```
byte __at (0x0) vidmem[152][256];
```

Writing both pixels in a byte is pretty easy:

```
vidmem[x][y] = 0x77;
```

---

[1] Except for Joust 2.

26. Williams Hardware

	$0000	$0100	$0200	
+00	7654 3210	7654 3210	7654 3210	....
01	7654 3210	7654 3210	7654 3210	....
02	7654 3210	7654 3210	7654 3210	....
03	7654 3210	7654 3210	7654 3210	....
04	7654 3210	7654 3210	7654 3210	....
05	7654 3210	7654 3210	7654 3210	....
06	7654 3210	7654 3210	7654 3210	....
07	7654 3210	7654 3210	7654 3210	....
..	....	....	....	....

Figure 26.2: Williams frame buffer pixel layout

If the colors are given separately, it can be done via bit-masking:

```
byte pixels = 0;
pixels |= (left_color << 4);      // set left pixel
pixels |= (right_color & 0xf);    // set right pixel
vidmem[x][y] = pixels;            // write to video memory
```

Setting an individual pixel already on the screen without affecting its neighbor is more complicated due to bank-switching. You'd have to locate your function in the upper ROM segment so you could safely read from the frame buffer. It would be just as easy to use the bit blitter chip for this, as we'll explain later.

26.5 Palette

Each of the 16 palette entries contains a single byte, mapped to RGB values like so:

```
Bit   76543210
Color BBGGGRRR
```

They live in a 16-byte array starting at address $C000:

```
byte __at (0xc000) palette[16];
```

You can convert separate red, green, and blue values (each 0-255) to a palette entry by shifting and masking bits:

```
inline void set_palette_rgb(byte i, byte red, byte green, byte
    blue) {
  byte n = 0;
  n |= red >> 5;
  n |= (green >> 2) & 0x38;
  n |= blue & 0xc0;
  palette[i] = n;
}
```

As an inline function, this won't take very much code at all if all parameters are constant values. To make it even simpler, you could pass a single word where each hex digit is an RGB component (all digits range from 0-7 except blue, which is 0-3):

```
inline void set_palette(byte i, word rgb) {
  byte n = 0;
  n |= (rgb >> 8) & 0x7;
  n |= (rgb >> 1) & 0x38;
  n |= (rgb << 6) & 0xc0;
  palette[i] = n;
}

set_palette(0, 0x000); // black
set_palette(1, 0x700); // red
set_palette(2, 0x773); // white
```

You could even use a macro — the format is identical to the Galaxian palette entries described in Chapter 17:

```
#define PE(r,g,b) ((r)|((g)<<3)|((b)<<6))
```

26.6 Bit Blitter

To use the bit blitter, you must first program all of its registers (there are only six) and write to the `flags` register last. This gives the "go" signal to the blitter. The CPU is halted, the blitter performs its task, and then the CPU is released.

26. Williams Hardware

Here is the basic process for performing a blit:

1. Set the **width and height** of the rectangle to be blitted. Each value is a byte, so the upper limit of each is 255. There is a special hack in the chip that makes a height of 255 act like 256, making it easier to draw a shape the entire height of the screen.
   There is also a bug in early Williams hardware that inverts the 3rd bit of the width and height registers. We've kept this bug, so instead of setting the register to width, you have to set it to width^4.
2. Set the **source address** (sstart), which tells the blitter where to copy from. (Solid rectangles can omit this step.) For sprites, you'd probably point to an array in ROM.
3. Set the **destination address** (dstart), which tells the blitter where to copy to. Usually this is somewhere within the frame buffer RAM.
4. Set the **solid color**, if the SOLID flag is set. Since there are two pixels per byte, this value represents the colors of two side-by-side pixels, making it easy to draw vertical patterns.
5. Set the appropriate **flags**, which also starts the blitter. There are eight flags:
   - SRCSCREEN: Set if the source is the video frame buffer. This should *not* be set when copying sprites from ROM — the blitter will then read bytes in row-major order (i.e., bytes are laid out row-by-row).
   - DSTSCREEN: Set if the destination is the video frame buffer. This should generally be set when copying from the screen, otherwise the blitter will write pixels sequentially, which, because of the video buffer layout, will smear pixels down the screen (might be useful for special effects!).
   - ESYNC: Also known as the SLOW flag. This must be set when making a RAM-to-RAM transfer, otherwise the video signal generator and the blitter chip will step on each other (technically known as "bus contention") and corrupt the data.

26.6. Bit Blitter

- FGONLY: Foreground Only. If set, any pixels with value 0 are not written. This makes it easy to do transparency.
- SOLID: Before writing to memory, the blitter replaces the data with a fixed color pattern (a two-pixel byte). If used in tandem with the transparency bit, this can be used to draw text or single-color sprites.
- RSHIFT: If set, shifts the source data one pixel to the right. Since every byte holds two pixels (4 bits each) this is useful for drawing to a rectangle starting at an odd-numbered X coordinate. (Pre-blitter games had two copies of each sprite, one copy shifted a single pixel to the right)
- EVENONLY: Only draw pixels with even X-coordinates (the upper 4 bits of each byte). Can be used to draw patterns, individual pixels, or special effects.
- ODDONLY: Only draw pixels with odd X-coordinates (the lower 4 bits of each byte).

In C, the blitter hardware registers are defined as follows:

```
// blitter flags
#define SRCSCREEN 0x1
#define DSTSCREEN 0x2
#define ESYNC 0x4
#define FGONLY 0x8
#define SOLID 0x10
#define RSHIFT 0x20
#define EVENONLY 0x40
#define ODDONLY 0x80

struct {
  byte flags;    // flags and 'go' signal
  byte solid;    // solid color (both nibbles)
  word sstart;   // source address
  word dstart;   // destination address
  byte width;    // width of rectangle
  byte height;   // height of rectangle
} __at (0xca00) blitter;
```

26. Williams Hardware

For ease of use, we've written some C functions to perform common blitter operations. First is a function to fill a rectangle with a solid color:

```
// x1: 0-151
// y1: 0-255
inline void blit_solid(byte x1, byte y1, byte w, byte h, byte
    color) {
  blitter.width = w^4;
  blitter.height = h^4;
  blitter.dstart = x1+y1*256; // swapped
  blitter.solid = color;
  blitter.flags = DSTSCREEN|SOLID;
}
```

For most of these functions, our X coordinate is byte-aligned, i.e., it only ranges from 0 to 151 and addresses even pixels. This is an acceptable compromise in some cases; in other cases, you'll want to have the full range of X coordinates available.

> The 6809 CPU has a *big-endian* byte order by default, which means the most significant byte comes first in address order. The Z80 is *little-endian*, and our emulator uses the 6809's byte ordering, so we have to swap the two bytes before writing to the 16-bit blitter registers sstart and dstart.

For the preceding function, we accomplish this just by swapping the X and Y coordinates in our calculation. For other cases, you can use this swapw function:

```
inline word swapw(word j) {
  return ((j << 8) | (j >> 8));
}
```

26.6. Bit Blitter

We'll use this for a function which copies data from ROM to a given rectangle on the screen while using transparency:

```
inline void blit_copy(byte x1, byte y1, byte w, byte h, const
    byte* data) {
  blitter.width = w^4;
  blitter.height = h^4;
  blitter.sstart = swapw((word)data);
  blitter.dstart = x1+y1*256; // swapped
  blitter.solid = 0;
  blitter.flags = DSTSCREEN|FGONLY;
}
```

Another approach is to embed the width (in pixel-pairs, i.e., pixel width/2) and height in the first two bytes of your sprite definition, like so:

```
const byte sprite1[] = {
  8,16,
  0x00,0x09,0x99,0x00,0x00,0x99,0x90,0x00,
  ...
};
```

Then draw your sprite like this, using just three parameters:

```
inline void draw_sprite(const byte* data, byte x, byte y) {
  blitter.width = data[0]^4;
  blitter.height = data[1]^4;
  blitter.sstart = swapw((word)(data+2));
  blitter.dstart = x+y*256; // swapped
  blitter.solid = 0;
  blitter.flags = DSTSCREEN|FGONLY;
}
```

26. Williams Hardware

26.7 Blitting to Pixel Boundaries

To put a single pixel on the screen with the blitter, just use the SOLID flag with a width and height of 1, and put the color index in both nibbles of the color argument:

```
inline void blit_pixel(word xx, byte y, byte color) {
  blitter.width = 1^4;
  blitter.height = 1^4;
  blitter.dstart = (xx>>1)+y*256; // swapped
  blitter.solid = color;
  blitter.flags = (xx&1) ? SOLID|ODDONLY : SOLID|EVENONLY;
}

blit_pixel(xx, y, 0x77);
```

Note that we're passing a 16-bit word as the X coordinate so we can address individual X coordinates from 0 to 303. We then set the EVENONLY or ODDONLY flag depending on whether X's first bit is set.

To draw a sprite at a pixel boundary, you can do something similar with the RSHIFT flag. It moves everything to the right 1 pixel. We can pass a 16-bit value for x and use bit 0 to determine whether or not to use the flag:

```
inline void draw_sprite2(const byte* data, word x, byte y) {
  blitter.width = data[0]^4;
  blitter.height = data[1]^4;
  blitter.sstart = swapw((word)(data+2));
  blitter.dstart = (x>>1) + y*256; // divide X by 2
  blitter.flags = (x&1) ? DSTSCREEN|FGONLY|RSHIFT :
    DSTSCREEN|FGONLY;
}
```

26.8 Other Hardware Locations

The switches and control inputs are located here:

```
volatile byte __at (0xc804) input0;
volatile byte __at (0xc806) input1;
volatile byte __at (0xc80c) input2;
```

The `rom_select` switch selects reading from ROM if set to 1, otherwise reads come from RAM (frame buffer):

```
byte __at (0xc900) rom_select;
```

The `video_counter` is a read-only location that returns the approximate scanline of the CRT electron beam (the lower two bits are always 0):

```
byte __at (0xcb00) video_counter;
```

If interrupts are enabled in the CPU, then an interrupt is generated four times per frame — on scanlines 0, 60, 188, and 252.

The watchdog needs to be reset by writing the exact value `0x39` at least once every 8 frames or the CPU will reset:

```
byte __at (0xcbff) watchdog0x39;
```

There's also 1024 bytes of non-volatile RAM for writing high scores and such:

```
byte __at (0xcc00) nvram[0x400];
```

26.9 When Not to Use memset()

On the Williams platform, we have the same problem using `memset` as in Chapter 17. Our bankswitching mode is set so that reads come out of ROM, so this routine dutifully copies the bytes in our ROM to the screen — leading to garbage bytes on the left-hand side.

Instead, use the blitter to clear the screen (a height value of 255 gets interpreted by the blitter as 256, so the entire screen is filled):

```
void clrscr() {
  blit_solid(0, 0, 152, 255, 0x00);
}
```

27

Williams Sprites

The Williams games, especially *Robotron: 2084*, were famous for their high sprite count and tricky video effects.

Even though the bit blitter helps with the heavy lifting of moving bytes to the frame buffer, a lot of work goes into making a responsive game that animates dozens of objects at 60 Hz.

 To see it on 8bitworkshop.com: Select the **Williams (Z80)** platform, then select the **Raster Paranoia Game** file.

27.1 Keeping Track of Objects

Our game has several different *linked lists* to keep track of different kinds of objects:

player_list - Contains just the player and a laser, when shot by the player. These are "fast" objects, updated once per frame.

fast_list - All other "fast" objects.

slow_lists - "Slow" objects are only updated once every 4 frames. This saves us some CPU time which can be used for other purposes. We have 4 separate lists and cycle between them.

effects_list - Exploding objects are moved here. Updated every frame.

obstacle_list - Objects which don't move at all.

free_list - A list of free Actor slots that can be used to spawn objects.

Each list is a *doubly-linked list*. Instead of each node just pointing to the next node, our nodes point to the next and previous node:

```
struct Actor* next;        // next in list
struct Actor** prevptr;    // pointer that points to us
```

Our "previous" pointer actually points to a pointer, not an Actor object directly. We do this because the first object in a list has no previous object — so we make the first object's prevptr point to the head pointer of the list. This makes it easy to remove objects without knowing which list contains it.

```
void add_actor(Actor** list, Actor* a) {
  // if this is not the first object,
  // rewrite existing head of list's prevptr
  if (*list) (*list)->prevptr = &a->next;
  // next pointer points to former head of list
  a->next = *list;
  // prev pointer points to head of list pointer
  a->prevptr = list;
  // update head of list pointer
  *list = a;
}

void remove_actor(Actor* a) {
  // if this is not the end of the list,
  // rewrite the next object's prevptr to bypass 'a'
  if (a->next) a->next->prevptr = a->prevptr;
  // rewrite the previous pointer to bypass 'a'
  *a->prevptr = a->next;
}
```

27.2 Getting Rid of Flicker

When a screen object is drawn or erased while the video generator is scanning over the object's portion of the video frame, *tearing artifacts* may be visible.

Figure 27.1: Doubly-linked list

To prevent this, we refresh the top and bottom section of the screen separately, using the video_counter byte to make sure they aren't currently being drawn:

```
effects_new_frame(); // restart effects list
// wait for beam to hit top half of screen
// (plus 16 pixels to accomodate max height of our sprites)
while (video_counter >= 0x90) effects_next();
// draw bottom half
update_screen_section(1);
// wait for beam to hit bottom half of screen
while (video_counter < 0x90) effects_next();
// draw top half
update_screen_section(0);
```

While we are waiting for video_counter to get to the right range, we run effects_next() to draw things like explosions. If we run out of time, no big deal, we'll get to it in the next frame.

The update_screen_section function draws the various lists of actors, only selecting objects that are in the top half or bottom half:

```
void update_actors_partial(Actor* a) {
  while (a) {
    if (g_section ^ (a->y < 0x80)) { // boolean XOR
      update_actor(a); // update actor
    }
    a = a->next; // next actor
  }
}

void update_screen_section(byte section) {
  g_section = section; // set global variable
  update_actors_partial(player_list);
  update_actors_partial(fast_list);
  update_actors_partial(slow_lists[frame & 3]);
}
```

27.3 Collision Detection

Detecting collisions becomes expensive in terms of CPU time when there are high numbers of objects flying around, so we try to run collision detection routines only when needed.

Our test_collision routine cycles through a list of actors, testing each against a rough *bounding box* using the *unsigned comparisons* we learned about in Chapter 20:

```
// assumes test_x and test_y
Actor* test_collisions(Actor* a) {
  while (a) {
    if ((byte)(test_y - a->y + 16) < 32 &&
        (byte)(test_x - a->x + 16) < 32 &&
        test_actor_pixels(a)) {
      return a; // collision found!
    }
    a = a->next;
  }
  return NULL; // no collision found
}
```

Any objects which pass the bounding box test move on to the test_actor_pixels function which performs a *pixel-accurate collision test*. We start by computing the intersection of the two bounding rectangles for each sprite being compared:

```
        byte x1 = maxbyte(test_actor->x, a->x);
        byte y1 = maxbyte(test_actor->y, a->y);
        byte x2 = minbyte(test_actor->x + test_actor->shape[0]*2,
                          a->x + a->shape[0]*2);
        byte y2 = minbyte(test_actor->y + test_actor->shape[1],
                          a->y + a->shape[1]);
        if (x2 <= x1 || y2 <= y1) return false;
```

27.3. Collision Detection

Figure 27.2: Intersection of two sprites' bounding boxes for collision test

If the intersection box is non-empty, we continue on to the pixel-by-pixel test. We only want to test pixels inside of the intersection box, so we do some complicated math to find the upper-left corner of each actor's pixel data. From that point, it's just a matter of looping over each pixel and seeing if any pixels collide:

```
    // pointers to upper-left corner of each actor's pixel data
    p1 = &test_actor->shape[2+(y1-test_actor->y) *
    test_actor->shape[0]];
    p1 += (x1 - test_actor->x) >> 1;
    p2 = &a->shape[2+(y1-a->y) * a->shape[0]];
    p2 += (x1 - a->x) >> 1;
    // loop over each pixel of intersection rectangle
    for (y=y1; y<y2; y++) {
      for (x=x1; x<x2; x++) {
        if (p1[x] && p2[x]) return true; // pixels collide
      }
      // move to next line of pixel data
      p1 += test_actor->shape[0];
      p2 += a->shape[0];
    }
  }
  return false; // no pixels collided
```

The collision routine does not inspect screen RAM; it uses only the sprite tables stored in ROM.

Note that a byte contains two pixels, so we'll detect a collision even if the left pixel is set in one sprite and the right pixel is set in the other. Good enough for our purposes!

27.4 Clipping

The blitter does not perform clipping (except on *Sinistar*, where the hardware supports an optional clipping window) so you can happily write past screen boundaries. Writing off the bottom side will wrap the sprite around to the top, shifted by one pixel. Writing off the right side, though, will probably chew up a bunch of your global variables.

A proper implementation of clipping would involve computing the intersection of the sprite rectangle with the screen rectangle, and only drawing pixels in the intersection – similar to what we did for the pixel collision test.

An easier solution is: Never write past the edges of the screen! In some places like the explosion rendering (draw_sprite_strided) we specifically prohibit writing past address $9000, just in case.

27.5 Getting By With 8 Bits

Our screen's width is 304 pixels, but a single byte can only cover 256 values. We want pixel accuracy for smooth animation, but we also want good performance. What's the compromise?

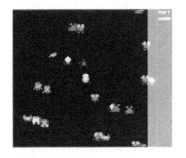

Figure 27.3: Screen width beyond 255 pixels

For performance reasons we decide to use 8-bit values for tracking objects' X and Y coordinates. Since most shapes are about 16 pixels wide, and there's a border around the screen, we only have 24 pixels to the side that are unused – we'll put the scoreboard there.

Our collision routine needs to be tweaked because computing the bounding box won't work if a coordinate overflows past 255. We'll handle this by clipping both X and Y coordinates to 255 (the right side and bottom side of the bounding box.)

28

Run-Length Encoding

 To see it on 8bitworkshop.com: Select the **Williams (Z80)** platform, then select the **RLE Bitmap** file.

The Williams hardware is capable of drawing quite large bitmaps. You are really only limited by the size of the ROM, which can only hold one uncompressed screen-sized bitmap. Unless you have some fancy bank-switching hardware, you might have to use data compression.

Most modern data compression methods, like those found in JPEG images or ZIP files, require a lot of memory and/or CPU time, but early methods still work fine. Run-length-encoding (RLE) is a simple method for compressing data that has long sequences of identical bytes. Bitmaps with solid colors often work well with RLE compression.

RLE breaks up data into packets of finite length. The first byte of the packet usually gives the length and the type of the packet — in our scheme, the high bit determines the type. A "run" packet outputs a string of identical bytes — for instance, this packet makes 7 copies of the byte $A5 (first byte is $87 since high bit is set):

87 A5

28. Run-Length Encoding

A "copy" packet just copies the bytes from the packet verbatim. For example, this packet outputs the numbers 1 through 5:

```
05 01 02 03 04 05
```

Since we are drawing images, we convert each byte into a pixel and draw them to the screen in a raster pattern (left-to-right, then up-to-down).

Getting a bitmap into RLE format is tricky, because the computing world has largely moved on to better compression techniques. The Truevision TGA format supports RLE encoding, and programs like ImageMagick convert into this format. It could be even more efficient if you repacked the data into 4 bits per pixel.

```
void draw_tga(const byte* tgadata, byte cenx, byte ceny) {
  const TGAHeader* hdr = (TGAHeader*) tgadata;
  const byte* src = hdr->data;
  byte* dest = &vidmem[cenx-hdr->width/4][ceny-hdr->height/2];
  byte i,j,lastbyte;
  // set palette from TGA
  for (i=0; i<8; i++) {
    byte pal = 0;
    pal |= (hdr->palette[i].r >> 5);
    pal |= (hdr->palette[i].g >> 2) & 0x38;
    pal |= (hdr->palette[i].b) & 0xc0;
    palette[i] = pal;
  }
  // iterate over height of image
  for (j=0; j<hdr->height; j++) {
    byte* start = dest;
    i = 0;
    lastbyte = 0;
    // iterate over width of image
    while (i<hdr->width) {
      byte count = *src++;
      byte rle = count & 0x80; // RLE has hi bit set
      byte color = 0;
      if (rle) {
        color = *src++; // fetch RLE byte
        count &= 0x7f; // discard hi bit
      }
      do {
        if (!rle)
          color = *src++; // no RLE, fetch raw data
        if ((i&1)==0) {
          *dest = lastbyte = (color << 4); // even byte
        } else {
          *dest = lastbyte | color; // odd byte
          dest += 256; // move right two pixels
        }
        i++;
      } while (count--);
    }
    dest = start+1; // next scanline
    watchdog0x39 = 0x39; // watchdog reset
  }
}
```

Figure 28.1: RLE-encoded TGA bitmap display routine

29

Williams Sound

Most of the sounds you hear in Williams games come from Eugene Jarvis, who developed the "Gwave" sound system while working on pinball games:

> Actually I started working with the Williams sound board on the pin *Lazer Ball*. On this game the memory was only 512 bytes for all program and data. It was this extreme memory crunch that inspired the Gwave wave table synthesizer. By storing a waveform (sine, square, triangle, etc.) in 4-64 bytes, and then a frequency table of 10-20 bytes, a sound could be characterized by a few bytes...I was stunned to find out that the most brilliant sounds were often created by typing in random numbers for the parameters.[11]

The Williams sound boards have their own Motorola 6800 CPU, attached to an 8-bit DAC (digital-to-analog-converter). The CPU shapes the waveform by changing the output of the DAC. The timing of the CPU determines the tone and frequency of the sound.

29. Williams Sound

29.1 The SWAVE System

 To see it on 8bitworkshop.com: Select the **Williams Sound (Z80)** platform, then select the **Wavetable Synth** file.

We're going to make our own primitive *wavetable* synthesizer in C. A wavetable is just an array of amplitude samples that we cycle through at varying frequencies to produce tones. The wavetable is responsible for the texture of the sound, or, more technically, its spectrum.

Our synth isn't identical to the Williams synth, since it uses a Motorola 6800, and we'll use an emulated Z80. But the concept is the same.

The sound CPU only has two I/O ports, one in and one out:

```
// command byte in
const __sfr __at (0x0) command;

// output sample to D/A converter
__sfr __at (0x0) dac;
```

The `main` routine starts by looking at the `command` port. If it's 0, we just zero out the DAC and `HALT` the CPU.

```
SoundEffect e;

void main() {
  if (command == 0) { dac = 0; HALT; }
  memcpy(&e, &SOUNDS[command], sizeof(e));
  play();
  HALT;
}
```

The `HALT` macro is inline assembly, and just generates the Z80 `HALT` instruction:

```
#define HALT __asm halt __endasm;
```

29.1. The SWAVE System

All of our sound generator's state will live in the `SoundEffect` struct:

```
typedef struct {
  word duration;       // duration of sound
  word offset;         // starting offset
  word delta;          // increments offset
  int deltainc;        // increments delta
  byte* wavetable;     // pointer to wavetable
  byte wavemask;       // mask for wavetable offset
  signed char lfo;     // increments deltainc
} SoundEffect;
```

The heart of the sound generator is the `sample` routine. This looks up a single sample in the wavetable based on the `offset` variable, then increments it with the `delta` parameter:

```
void sample() {
  byte val = e.wavetable[(byte)(e.offset >> 8) & e.wavemask];
  if (val <= volume) dac = val; // output sample, if <= volume
  e.offset += e.delta;
}
```

Our `play` routine loads the appropriate wavetable pointer into the `wav` variable, then loops until `duration` decrements to zero. We call `sample` eight times in the loop — this is sometimes called *unrolling the loop*.

```
void play() {
  wav = &WAVES[e.wavetable];
  while (e.duration--) {
    sample();
    sample();
    sample();
    sample();
    sample();
    sample();
    sample();
    sample();
    e.delta += e.deltainc;
    e.deltainc += e.lfo;
    // taper off volume near end of sound
    if (e.duration <= 0xff) volume = e.duration;
  }
}
```

An advantage of unrolling the loop is that we update slow-moving values like duration and delta less often, effectively increasing their precision.

29.2 Triggering Sounds from the Main CPU

When the main CPU wants to play a new sound, it sends a single byte command to the sound board over its *PIA (peripheral interface adapter)* port. This immediately resets the sound CPU, and its sound program can now read the byte and figure out what to do. (This is why in Williams games you never near more than one sound at a time!)

```
byte __at (0xc80e) sound_pia;    // sound PIA

sound_pia = 0x3f;                // prepare sound board
sound_pia = sound_command;       // send sound command
```

Because some sounds are more important than others, Williams games have a priority system where lower-priority sounds are squelched until higher-priority sounds have finished playing. The CPU can keep a table of durations to estimate how long a particular sound should play before it can be interrupted.

In the 8bitworkshop emulator, the sound ROM must be placed at a certain location at memory. The emulator will detect it and load it into the virtual sound board.

```
const byte __at(0x9000) SOUND_ROM[] = {
0xdb,0x00,0xb7,0x20,0x01,0x76,0x11 .....
};
```

To download the sound ROM, go to the "Williams Sound (Z80)" target and select "Download ROM Image". There is an example of converting the ROM image to C array format in the williams/ directory of the 8bitworkshop Tools (see Chapter 30.)

30

Importing Assets

Writing games requires lots of *assets*, like bitmaps, fonts, and music scores. In the old days, this was done by drawing pixels on graph paper and building lists of bytes by hand. Fortunately, we now have better tools at our disposal (although the old way is straightforward!).

The 8bitworkshop IDE is mainly about code, so we leave the graphics editing to better-suited tools. We've also written some conversion utilities of our own that'll make it easier.

30.1 Installing 8bitworkshop Tools

The 8bitworkshop Tools require Python 2.x and ImageMagick. Before downloading the tools themselves, you'll want to get your environment ready. We've provided instructions for Ubuntu Linux and Windows 10.

Installing 8BitWorkshop Tools on Ubuntu Linux

1. First, install python, python-pip, and ImageMagick:

   ```
   $ sudo apt update
   $ sudo apt install python python-pip imagemagick
   ```

2. If you plan to convert MIDI files, you'll need the `mido` package. You can install this using the `pip` command:

   ```
   $ sudo pip install mido
   ```

3. Next, download the tools:

   ```
   $ wget
       http://8bitworkshop.com/release/8bitworkshop-tools.tgz
   ```

4. Extract the tools:

   ```
   $ tar -xzvf 8bitworkshop-tools.tgz
   ```

5. The tools will be extracted to the 8bitworkshop-tools directory. Type the following to move into the directory and list its contents:

   ```
   $ cd 8bitworkshop-tools && ls
   ```

6. To see example usage of the tools, move into each directory and run make; for example:

   ```
   $ cd williams && make
   ```

Installing 8BitWorkshop Tools on Windows 10

Windows 10 provides a Linux-based subsystem (running Ubuntu) you can use to download and use 8bitworkshop tools.

1. Open **Settings**, select **Update and Security**, select For Developers, then enable the **Developer Mode** radio button.
2. When prompted, select **Yes**.
3. After installation is complete, open the Control Panel, select **Programs** and, under **Programs and Features**, select **Turn Windows Features On or Off**.
4. Scroll down to **Windows Subsystem for Linux (beta)**, enable its checkbox, then click **OK**.
5. You'll be prompted to reboot your computer. Reboot and, after it restarts, type **bash** in your search field and Bash will open.
   You'll have to wait several minutes for it to install and unpack itself.
6. When prompted, enter a new username and password for your Linux account on your system.
7. Install python and ImageMagick:

30.1. Installing 8bitworkshop Tools

```
$ sudo apt install python python-pip imagemagick
```

8. If you plan to convert MIDI files, install `mido`:

```
$ sudo pip install mido
```

9. By default, when you first connect to the Windows Linux-based subsystem, you're placed in the System 32 directory. We don't want to put our tools there, so let's move back to our home directory:

```
$ cd ~/
```

10. Next, download the tools:

```
$ wget
    http://8bitworkshop.com/release/8bitworkshop-tools.tgz
```

11. Extract the tools:

```
$ tar -xzvf 8bitworkshop-tools.tgz
```

12. The tools will be extracted to the `8bitworkshop-tools` directory. Type the following to move into the directory and list its contents:

```
$ cd 8bitworkshop-tools && ls
```

13. To see example usage of the tools, move into each directory and run make; for example:

```
$ cd williams && make
```

Installing 8BitWorkshop Tools on Mac OS

Python is installed on MacOS by default, but you will want to install ImageMagick and, if you're planning on editing MIDI files, install `mido`. To install ImageMagick, you'll want to download MacPorts if you don't already have it installed on your system. (You can also use Homebrew.)

1. Install Xcode. See `https://guide.macports.org/#installing.xcode` for full instructions specific to your MacOS version.

30. Importing Assets

2. Download and install the MacPorts binary. Links to binaries for each version of MacOS are available at
   `https://www.macports.org/install.php`
3. Install ImageMagick:

   ```
   $ sudo port install ImageMagick
   ```

4. If you plan to convert MIDI files, install `mido`:

   ```
   $ sudo pip install mido
   ```

5. Next, download the tools:

   ```
   $ wget
       http://8bitworkshop.com/release/8bitworkshop-tools.tgz
   ```

6. Extract the tools:

   ```
   $ tar -xzvf 8bitworkshop-tools.tgz
   ```

7. The tools will be extracted to the `8bitworkshop-tools` directory. Type the following to move into the directory and list its contents:

   ```
   $ cd 8bitworkshop-tools && ls
   ```

8. To see example usage of the tools, move into each directory and run make; for example:

   ```
   $ cd williams && make
   ```

30.2 Graphics Tools

parsebdf8.py - Converts a Bitmap Distribution Format (BDF) font file to be used in tile-based graphics. BDF fonts are not very common, but are used in X Windows.

parsebdf4bit.py - Converts a BDF font to be used in Williams games.

pbm_to_c.py - Converts a Portable Bitmap (PBM) to a monochrome sprite format for the Midway 8080 platform.

pcx2will.py - Converts a PCX bitmap file to a sprite definition for Williams games.

30.3 Sound Tools

mknotes.py - Finds the best base frequency for a given range of notes, then generates a table of period values for the PSG.

midi2song.py - Converts a MIDI file to a song file, as described in Chapter 19.

Most of the above tools have an example of their usage – look at the Makefile in each `tools/<platform>` directory.

30.4 Third-Party Tools

You may find third party tools useful for asset creation.

Gimp - The standard Linux graphics editor.

8x8 Pixel ROM Font Editor - A Windows editor for 8x8 bitmap fonts. Exports assembler code that could be massaged into C arrays.

https://www.min.at/prinz/o/software/pixelfont/

Turaco - An older DOS program that can edit ROMs of many different arcade platforms, including Galaxian-format graphics ROMs. The DOS version runs under the DOSBox emulator; there is also a command-line version (`turacocl`) that builds on multiple platforms.

http://umlautllama.com/projects/turaco/

Allegro Sprite Editor (aseprite) - A popular pixel editor. An older free version (0.9.5) is available for download; it's also in the aseprite package on Ubuntu.

https://www.aseprite.org/older-versions/

30.5 Free Art

https://opengameart.org/ has many freely-licensed sprite files. Search for "8x8" or "16x16" to find results.

30. IMPORTING ASSETS

30.6 Using 8bitworkshop Offline

You can use the 8bitworkshop IDE offline, too. Just download the latest release from here:

`http://8bitworkshop.com/release/`

Unpack it, then open the `index.html` file in Firefox and start editing. All code changes will be persisted to your browser's local storage, so clearing your browser's cache or resetting it may clear the storage. Make sure to save your edited files elsewhere.

31

Distributing Your Game

Now that you've put hours of work into designing, developing, playtesting, and tweaking your game, it's time to share it with the world!

In the 8bitworkshop IDE, choose the "Share File" menu item in the IDE to generate a shareable web link. Anyone opening this link will see the source code and will be able to play the emulated game in the browser. (Note: This will publish your source code to the Internet.)

31.1 Making ROM Files

For certain platforms, you can also play your game on arcade game emulators like *MAME*. For non-Z80 platforms you would have to develop your game in assembly — a topic outside the scope of this book, although the IDE has 6502 and 6809 assemblers.

Platform	8bitworkshop ID	MAME driver	Language
VIC Dual	vicdual	carnival	C/Z80 asm
Galaxian	galaxian	galaxian	C/Z80 asm
Scramble	galaxian-scramble	scramble	C/Z80 asm
Atari B&W Vector	vector-ataribw	asteroid	6502 ASM
Atari Color Vector	vector-ataricolor	bwidow	6502 ASM
Williams	williams	robotron	6809 ASM

Table 31.1: MAME support for 8bitworkshop platforms

31. Distributing Your Game

Choose the "Download ROM Image" menu item to download a ROM image of your compiled game.

To convert it into a MAME archive, first go into the 8bitworkshop-tools directory we downloaded in Chapter 30 for your target platform:

```
$ cd vicdual
$ python rom_carnival.py [your rom image]

$ cd scramble
$ python rom_scramble.py [your rom image]
```

This will split your ROM image into individual ROM files, producing a ZIP file to be used in MAME. You can start MAME from the command line, using the -rompath setting to tell it where to find your custom ZIP file, e.g.:

```
wine mame64.exe -window -rompath
    ~/8bitworkshop-tools/scramble/ scramble
```

It will complain about "wrong checksums" – that's good, that means it found your custom ROM file! Remember that the sound boards are not faithfully reproduced in the 8bitworkshop emulator, so you probably won't have sound unless you went above and beyond.

31.2 Playing on Actual Hardware

If you're lucky enough to have a functional arcade cabinet, you could (in theory) replace its ROMs with your own game. This is also outside the scope of this book (we haven't tried it!) but we'll go over some possibilities.

The most straightforward technique is to get an EPROM Eraser and an EPROM Programmer, burn your own *EPROM*s, and replace the ones in the arcade PCB. You can often replace all of the separate ROMs with a single EPROM (there are instructions for several machines at http://cambridgearcade.dyndns.org/).

31.2. Playing on Actual Hardware

Another possibility is to connect a Raspberry Pi (or a fast microcontroller) to the address and data bus of the PCB, and write a program to "bit-bang" the data onto the bus from the Pi's GPIO ports. This has been done with some success for Atari 2600 cartridges.

If you know how to program an FPGA board, you could in theory replace the RAM, ROM, CPU, sound and video generation logic. Or just write an software emulator to do the same thing. Or just get a PC running AdvanceMame and stick it in the arcade chassis (See where this leads...?)

Figure 31.1: Raspberry Pi Zero, a tiny $5 computer which is 1000x more powerful than the Galaxian arcade system board shown in the preface of this book (photo by Gareth Halfacree, CC BY-SA 2.0)

Appendix A: Troubleshooting

Programmer Error

Programming is hard. Programming in C is harder. Programming in C with a web-based IDE and dodgy debugging support? That's just crazy! :) Anyway, here are some common things that go wrong:

Forgetting to set the stack pointer

If you find that your program crashes soon after it starts, you may have just forgotten to set the stack pointer in your entry routine! See Chapter 6.

Forgetting to initialize data

If you find that global variables are zero or not the values you expect, you may have forgotten to set up the initialized data segment in your entry routine! See Chapter 16.

Writing outside of array boundaries

C does not have array boundary checking, so it will happily write to memory outside of arrays if you tell it to. This can easily overwrite your variables in RAM. Make sure you check array accesses, especially when drawing sprites.

Expressions don't work as expected

C has lots of *operator precedence* rules that can be confusing. When in doubt, add parentheses. You may also have to cast your expression to a signed or unsigned value – see Chapter 20.

Infinite linked lists or corrupt objects

Getting pointers right when using linked lists is tricky. Make sure you don't keep a pointer to an object after calling free() on an object you've malloc()'ed. Consider also whether you would prefer to use a simpler data structure, like an array.

Appendix A: Troubleshooting

Compiler Oddities

The SDCC compiler is under active development as of 2017, but sometimes you find a compiler bug. (Some of these bugs might even be fixed by the time you read this!)

Non-fatal Compiler Internal Problem in file ... line number '1018' : Definition not found

The following code generates this cryptic error message:

```
const byte* e = "HELLO";
while (*e >= 0) {          // condition always true
   *e++;
}
```

The problem is that e is a byte pointer, which is a type alias for unsigned char, and thus the expression *e >= 0 is always true. This messes with the loop induction optimizer and it spits forth a confusing message. The solution is to remove the offending expression, or change it so that it isn't always true.

inline functions don't always work

If you encounter different behavior with the inline keyword than without it, you might have found a bug in the compiler.

char is unsigned by default

SDCC makes the char type unsigned by default. This is not a bug so much as a deviation from the majority of C compilers. We use byte and sbyte in our example code, except in cases where the sign doesn't matter.

Bibliography

[1] Zilog Z80. https://en.wikipedia.org/wiki/Zilog_Z80.

[2] Kevin Smith. The Ultimate (So-Far) History of Gremlin Industries. http://allincolorforaquarter.blogspot.com/2015/09/the-ultimate-so-far-history-of-gremlin_25.html.

[3] Dr. H. Holden. ATARI PONG E CIRCUIT ANALYSIS & LAWN TENNIS: BUILDING A DIGITAL VIDEO GAME WITH 74 SERIES TTL IC's. http://www.pong-story.com/.

[4] General Instrument. AY-3-8910 Data Sheet. http://map.grauw.nl/resources/sound/generalinstrument_ay-3-8910.pdf.

[5] The Dot Eaters. Gun Fight and Nutting Associates - Hired Guns. http://thedoteaters.com/?bitstory=gun-fight-and-nutting-associates.

[6] Simon Parkin. The Space Invader. *The New Yorker*, 2013.

[7] Tristan Donovan. *Replay: The History of Video Games*. 2010.

[8] shmuplations. Galaga 30th Anniversary Developer Interview. http://shmuplations.com/galaga/.

[9] Bill Paul. The History of Cinematronics, Inc. http://zonn.com/Cinematronics/history.htm.

[10] Jed Margolin. The Secret Life of XY Monitors. http://www.jmargolin.com/xy/xymon.htm.

[11] Interview with Eugene Jarvis. http://www.firepowerpinball.com/downloads/Eugene_Jarvis_Interview.pdf.

Bibliography

[12] I got to meet Eugene Jarvis and Sam Dicker! https://my-cool-projects.blogspot.com/2014/07/i-got-to-meet-eugene-jarvis-and-sam.html.

[13] Sean Riddle. Blitter Information. http://seanriddle.com/blitter.html.

[14] Larry DeMar. *Retro Gamer*, (80), 2013.

Some content is licensed under a Creative Commons license: https://creativecommons.org/licenses/

Index

8-bit architecture, 1
8bitworkshop.com, 33

address bus, 6
addressing mode, 7, 12
Analog Vector Generator, 147
areas, 105
array initializer, 160
arrays
    indexing, 45
assembler, 7
assembly language, 7
assembly listing, 22
assets, 211

base 16, 2
BCD, 71
big-endian, 192
binary notation, 1
binary-coded decimal, 71
bit, 1
bit blitter, 186
bit field, 89
bit fields, 89
bitmask, 47, 60
bitplanes, 116
bitwise operators, 31
boolean inversion, 48
bounding box, 173, 200
branch, 14
byte, 1

C compiler, 35
case, 158
cells, 38
clipping, 80

clock cycle, 5
color palette, 41
const, 105
constant folding, 70
CPU clock, 5

Dangling pointers, 169
data bus, 5
data segment, 27
data structures, 88
debugger, 35
declaration, 21
dereferencing, 74
Digital Vector Generator, 147
doubly-linked list, 198
dynamic memory, 168

edges, 159
empty statement, 46
emulator, 35, 78
entropy, 103
entry routine, 25
exclusive-or, 58

fixed-point, 120
fixups, 24
flags, 13
floating-point, 182
frame buffer, 77
function, 20
function call, 21
Function pointers, 171
function signature, 171
function type, 171

games

v

Index

Asteroids, 145, 146
Asteroids Deluxe, 177
Battlezone, 155, 161, 177
Blockade, 37, 51
Carnival, 38, 47, 48
Checkmate, 37
Computer Space, 65
Crazy Kong, 110
Defender, 185
Donkey Kong, vi, 110
Flight Simulator, 155
Fonz, 155
Frogger, vi, 109
Galaga, 109
Galaxian, vi, 109, 110, 116
Gee Bee, 109
Gun Fight, 77
Head On, 38
Joust, 186
King & Balloon, 109
Lazer Ball, 207
LEM, 145
Lunar Lander, vi, 145
Night Driver, 155
Pac-Man, vi, 38
Play Ball, 37
Pong, 65
Red Baron, 155, 161
Robotron, 186
Robotron: 2084, 186, 197
Safari, 38
Scramble, 109–111, 114, 116
Siege, 51, 52
Sinistar, 202
Solarian, 119
Space Invaders, vi, vii, 77, 78, 100, 109, 185
Space Wars, 145
Spacewar, 145
Star Raiders, 177
Star Wars, vi, 109, 146
Tempest, vi, 146
Trapshoot, 37
Tron, 37
VEC9, 146
global namespace, 165
global variables, 27, 168
GPU, 83
grows downward, 16

header files, 20
heap, 168, 169
hexadecimal notation, 2
hidden line removal, 164

IDE, 33
    debugging, 36
identifier, 21
identity matrix, 157
incomplete type, 171
index register, 11
initialized, 106
initializers, 160
inline assembly, 49, 98
integer conversion rules, 143
integer overflow, 4
integer promotion, 143
interrupts, 97
    mode 0, 97
    mode 2, 132

Index

jump, 14

library function, 24
line comment, 21
linear-feedback shift
    register, 101
    Galois, 101
linked list, 168, 169
linked lists, 197
little-endian, 7, 13, 192
local variable, 29
local variables, 45, 168
logical operators, 31

machine code, 7
macro definitions, 20
macro expansion, 20
main(), 45
main() function, 44
MAME, 217
Manhattan distance, 173
memory allocation, 168
memset, 117
memset() function, 45
modulus, 4, 124
multi-line comments, 21

namespaces, 165
nibbles, 2
null terminator, 75

object code, 23
object scale, 166
opcode, 7
operand, 7
operator associativity, 183
operator precedence, i, 183

PCB, 9

period, 101
peripheral interface
    adapter, 210
PIA, 210
pipeline, 19
pixel-accurate collision test,
    200
platforms, vi
pointer, 73, 79
pointer arithmetic, 76, 94
preprocessor, 20
preprocessor directive, 20
prerendering, 163
primitive types, 43
Program Counter, 11
PROM, 43, 113, 218
pseudorandom number
    generator, 101

radius test, 173
raster scan, 146
registers, 5, 10
relational operator, 29
relocatable, 23
return type, 21
Running out of memory,
    169

screen scale, 166
seed, 101
segments, 105
short-circuit evaluation, 31,
    175
sign extension, 142
signed, 3
signed vs. unsigned, 3
stack allocation, 168
stack frame, 16

vii

Index

Stack Pointer, 11
standard library, 45
static allocation, 168
struct, 52
struct initializer, 170
struct initializers, 160
switch statement, 158

tag namespace, 165
tearing artifacts, 198
tiles, 38
truncated, 4
two's complement, 3
type cast, 73, 130, 169
typedef, 43

uninitialized, 105
union, 181
unrolling the loop, 209
unsigned, 3
unsigned comparisons, 200
untyped, 169
user-defined types, 43

variable, 27
vector monitor, 146
vertices, 159
volatile, 83

watchdog, 85
wavetable, 208
wireframe models, 159

Z80
    logical operations, 17
    shift operations, 61

Made in the USA
Coppell, TX
13 August 2022